RAW FOOD SALAD BAR
SIMPLE SOUPS AND SALADS

By **Philip McCluskey**

AUTHOR OF
RAW FOOD, FAST FOOD

WWW.LOVINGRAW.COM   LOVINGRAW, LLC - CT

2010

Lovingraw, LLC
Danbury, CT 06810

Copyright © 2010 by Philip McCluskey

ISBN 1451591632
EAN-13 9781451591637

All rights reserved. No part of this publication may be reproduced in any form or by an means, electronic or mechanical, including photocopying, recording, or any other information storage and retrieval system, without the written permission of the author.

Printed in the United States

COVER DESIGNER / LAYOUT: Nicole Byrkit
COVER PHOTOGRAPHY: Jeff Skeirik
ALL OTHER PHOTOGRAPHY: Jenny Nelson
EDITOR: Gena Hamshaw

For more information visit:
www.lovingraw.com
www.rawfoodsaladbar.com

DISCLAIMER

This book and any information contained herein is not intended to replace a diagnosis from anyone in the medical profession, to cure any illness, disease or health problem. All information is based on personal experience and in the case of any health condition, please seek medical help.

TABLE OF CONTENTS

Vegetable Salads:

Balsamic Bitter Greens...4

A Salad And Two Dressings..5

Sweet and Sour Greens...7

Avocado, Honey and Dandelion Greens...8

Shredded Kale with Veggies..9

Herbs & Olives Salad...10

Beets, Carrots, and Radish with Arugula......................................11

Herb Coleslaw...12

Herb and Endive Shaved Salad...13

Chive & Sage Salt..14

Mesclun, Sungold and Kalamata Olive Mash...............................15

Heirloom Tomato Salad..16

Sungolds and Green Beans Tossed with Herbs............................17

Cucumber, Radish and Sungold Salsa with Mint.........................18

Tomato and Fennel Plate..19

Avocado Corn Relish...20

Sweet Chipotle Marinated Mushroom Steak over Mixed Greens...21

Avocado and Onion Slices..23

Tomato Coulis over a Bed of Mesclun..24

Scarlett O'Hara Bowl..25

Earth and Sea (Salad)...26

Orange and White Salad...27

White and Black..28

Cucumbers and Coconut Cream..29

Autumn & Winter Salads:

Dragon Slaw..32

Marinated Celery...33

French Bistro Remoulade..34

Apple Parsnip Autumn Salad..35

Spicy Sweet Slaw..36

Nordic Winter Salad..37

Mistaken Identity Salad..38

Sweet Potato, Cauliflower & Tomato Salad....................................39

Marinated Raw Beet Salad with Basil...40

Sweet Baby Brussels Blend...41

Carrot and Poppy Seed Salad with Cream Sauce..........................42

Gingered Dragon Bowl of Broccoli..43

Pesto Salad..45

Delhi Carrots..45

Mixed Bok Choy...47

Courgette Ribbon Salad..48

Fruit Salads:

Endless Summer Fruit Salad..50

Young Thai Coconut Bowl..51

Green Tang Salad...52

Sweet Celeriac (slaw)..53

Shades of Red and Pink..54

Minted Basil & Citrus Melon..55

Purple, Green and Yellow Salad..56

Avocado and Grapefruit with Pepitas and Coconut..................57

Rubies and Emeralds (Spinach and Strawberry Salad)............58

Balsamic Strawberries and Brunost with Arugula...................59

Morning Glory Salad..60

Minted Peaches, Corn Salsa & Smoky Mesquite Sauce over Mixed Greens...61

Creamy Comfort Soups:

Marrakesh Express..66

Rosemary Pea Soup...67

Silky Spinach with Strands of Dulse..68

Mushroom Ginger Stew...69

Mexican Cream..70

Avocado & Chipotle Bisque...71

Spiced Parsnip Soup..72

Southern Belles in London Soup..73

Spicy Blonde..74

Smokey Mushroom Mesquite Soup...75

Winter Pear..76

New Garlic Soup..77

Cajun Creole..78

Bloody Mary Soup...79

Shiitake Sweet and Sour..81

Picadillo Soup..82

Jamaican Stew..84

Winter Warming Chili..85

Avocado Soup..86

Summer Cooler Soups:

Gazpacho with Cumin and Avocado..88

Summer Minestrone..89

Chilled Zucchini Soup..90

Corn, Avocado and Basil Chowder..91

Fresh Berry Soup..92

Tomato Basil Soup..93

Sweet Chilled Avocado Cucumber and Paprika Soup..............94

August Sunset..95

Additional Info:

Ingredients..97

References..110

Notes..111

Sources..113

Book Recommendations..114

v

INTRODUCTION

I hear it time and time again from those who are new to raw foods: "is all you eat salads?"

The answer is most definitely no! As a raw foods chef, motivational speaker, author, and blogger, I've devoted my career to showing those who are interested in raw foods, but whose culinary tastes go beyond greens and fruit, that a raw diet can offer just as much fulfillment and satiety as a standard American diet—and more. It offers true nourishment, and the satisfaction of knowing that you're doing the planet a service with every local, organic, and plant-based bite. Most of all it offers a healthy, thriving, balanced body.

Even at its most nourishing and hearty, raw food preparation doesn't have to be time consuming, expensive, or complex. In my last book, Raw Food, Fast Food, I show readers that even the most filling raw meals can take about ten minutes from start to finish to prepare. Ten Minutes! I'll bet thats only a fraction of the time you're used to spending sautéing, grilling, steaming, searing, roasting, and baking. So to answer the time-honored salad question: no, we don't just eat salads.

This said, the raw lifestyle is just like any other lifestyle in that one isn't always in the mood to whip up a special meal. Sometimes, all we want is a simple, basic standby. And this is where salads enter the spotlight. Salads and soups, which are the stars of this cookbook, are the staples of a raw foodist's everyday diet. They're certainly not the only things we eat, but I'm guessing that if you surveyed most raw foodists, you'd find that a salad creeps in most days.

Think of them as our version of spaghetti, or roast chicken, or any other dish that you're used to eating for dinner a few times weekly: they're the standbys that we return to again and again for joy and nourishment.

But standbys don't have to be boring. In Raw Food Salad Bar, I've done my best to show you that the best salads are anything but! With a few simple variations in flavor, ingredients, and dressing, salads offer up nothing short of a world of possibility. Think of them as canvases on which you can paint almost anything you want, and my recipes as a hint of inspiration. The same goes for soups. The soups in this book go far beyond comfort food. From the simple and elegant to the spicy and complex, there is a raw soup to suit any mood. There's only one common denominator: they're all quick, easy to prepare, and totally delicious.

It's my hope that this book will show you that even the basic building blocks of a raw diet offer you tremendous versatility and flavor. All you need is some delicious organic produce, a few spare minutes of time, and lots of love to prepare a perfect meal. Get blending and chopping, and enjoy!

Philip McCluskey
March, 2010

PART I: SALADS

A GUIDE TO GREENS:

It's best to layer flavors and textures in salads, so that they dance around in your mouth in all of their variety!

Get creative. Don't be afraid to play with combinations of bitter, sweet, tender, pungent, and spicy. Mother Nature has provided these flavors and sensations in a garden fresh array, and with all the nutrients and health benefits we need. Enjoy the wealth!

FOR THE DIFFERENT TASTES, USE:

Tangy: Endive (or frisee)

Bitter: Escarole, endive, radicchio, dandelion, any chicory

Tart: Escarole, dandelion

Peppery: Radicchio

Sweet/Tangy/Bitter: Mesclun mix

Spicy: Mustard greens

All members of the chicory family and any spring harvested green (like dandelion or nettles) work well with sweet additions, like raisins, sun-dried tomatoes, dates, honey dressings, basil, miso, and even nuts.

VEGETABLE SALADS

BALSAMIC BITTER GREENS

Calling something bitter makes it sound as if it shouldn't be appetizing at all, right?

Au contraire. It's heaven.

INGREDIENTS

ARUGULA, RADICCHIO, DANDELION GREENS, ENDIVE, ANY GREEN THAT'S LOCAL AND IN SEASON, MIXED TOGETHER AND GATHERED INTO JUST UNDER TWO GENEROUS HANDFULS PER SERVING

DIRECTIONS

Toss with a generous amount of balsamic vinegar and a spoonful of raw honey or agave, the tiniest bit of cold pressed oil (your choice), coarse sea salt and black pepper, with a sprinkle of nutritional yeast over the entire mix.

A SALAD AND TWO DRESSINGS:

For the base in these two salad variations, simply use your favorite mix of greens. Top with either of the two dressings, and see for yourself how the mere change in a salad dressing can provide delightful contrast between meals. It's all in the dressing!

Green Gods and Goddesses Dressing

INGREDIENTS
1 AVOCADO
1 BUNCH CHOPPED SCALLIONS
1 HANDFUL CILANTRO
1 TABLESPOON MINT LEAVES
1/4 CUP HEMP SEEDS OR 2 HEAPING TABLESPOONS OF HEMP BUTTER
2 TABLESPOONS APPLE CIDER VINEGAR
1 TABLESPOON COLD PRESSED OIL
   JUST ENOUGH WATER TO BLEND (ADD SLOWLY AS YOU DO UNTIL DESIRED CONSISTENCY, KEEPING IN MIND THAT IT WILL SOLIDIFY IN THE FRIDGE)
   SALT AND PEPPER (TO TASTE)

DIRECTIONS

1. Shake all ingredients in a mason jar, (add slowly as you do until desired consistency) and season with salt and pepper to taste.
2. Serve over mixed greens.

Honey Mustard Dressing

INGREDIENTS

2 TABLESPOONS RAW HONEY, OR AGAVE IF YOU'D RATHER NOT USE HONEY
1 TABLESPOON APPLE CIDER VINEGAR
1 TABLESPOON EXTRA VIRGIN, COLD-PRESSED OLIVE OIL
1 TABLESPOON ORGANIC DIJON OR STONEGROUND MUSTARD
   (FREE OF PRESERVATIVES)

DIRECTIONS

1. Shake and season to taste in a mason jar.
2. Serve over mixed greens.

SWEET AND SOUR GREENS

Since this is shaken up in a mason (or any glass) jar with a lid, it's easy as can be, and it's especially fun for kids to help with.

INGREDIENTS
1 TABLESPOON RAW HONEY (OR AGAVE)
JUICE OF 1 LEMON
1 TABLESPOON FRESH SQUEEZED ORANGE JUICE
1 TABLESPOON BRAGG'S AMINO ACIDS OR NAMA SHOYU
A GENEROUS PINCH OF SEA SALT
FRESH GROUND BLACK PEPPER AND A PINCH OF NUTMEG

DIRECTIONS
1. Shake all ingredients together and splash over a huge bowl or individual plates of mixed greens.

AVOCADO, **HONEY** AND **DANDELION** GREENS

The creamy avocado and sweet honey cuts down on the bitterness of dandelion greens in this salad. (Can you believe something so delicious and powerful for your health is considered a pesky weed??) Harvesting the greens early in the spring also helps lessen the bite.

INGREDIENTS

- **2** AVOCADOS, PITTED AND SLICED
- **1** TABLESPOON RAW HONEY
- **6** CUPS DANDELION GREENS, WASHED AND CHOPPED
- SALT AND PEPPER (TO TASTE)
- **1** PINCH CHIPOTLE PEPPER

DIRECTIONS

1. Massage the dandelion greens with the honey for a few minutes, thinking lovely and delicious thoughts.
2. Add the avocados.
3. Season with salt and pepper and a pinch of chipotle pepper before serving.

SHREDDED **KALE** WITH **VEGGIES**

Shredded kale salads are dietary staples for most raw foodists. Here, the kale is paired with two vegetable counterparts—carrot and jicama—that give it an earthy, yet light and bright, presentation.

INGREDIENTS
1 HEAD KALE
1/2 OF A JICAMA, PEELED AND CHOPPED
2 CARROTS, CHOPPED
2 TABLESPOONS APPLE CIDER VINEGAR
JUICE OF 1 LEMON
1 TABLESPOON RAW HONEY (OR AGAVE)
COARSE SEA SALT, TO TASTE
RAW NUTS (OPTIONAL GARNISH—I LIKE BRAZIL NUTS WITH THIS COMBINATION)

DIRECTIONS

1. Pulse the kale, jicama, and carrots quickly in a food processor, or finely chop with a knife.
2. Hand-toss together with the vinegar, lemon, honey and sea salt.
3. Add the raw nuts and either serve immediately or let it "marinate" for a bit (either at room temperature or in the fridge if it's going to be a few hours).

HERBS&OLIVES SALAD

Elegant and simple. Perfect for a solitary meal, or make more for a crowd.

INGREDIENTS

- **1** LARGE HANDFUL OF ARUGULA PER SERVING
- **1** LARGE FENNEL BULB (OR 2 IF THEY'RE SMALLER), FEATHERY GREEN TOPS TAKEN OFF WITH A HANDFUL KEPT FOR GARNISH, COARSE OUTSIDE DISCARDED, SLICED INTO THIN PIECES
- **1** BUNCH FRESH BASIL (TRY THE LEMON VARIETY FOR DIFFERENT FLAVORS)
- **1** HANDFUL OF FRESH DILL, FINELY MINCED
- **1** RED CHILI THINLY SLICED AND SEEDED (OR DRIED CHILI FLAKES)
- **1** HANDFUL MARJORAM LEAVES (FRESH), FINELY DICED OR 1 TABLESPOON DRIED
- **1** CUP SUN-DRIED OLIVES (BLACK OR GREEN OR A MIX, I LOVE SUNFOOD'S PERUVIAN OLIVES BEST)
  COARSE SEA SALT AND FRESH BLACK PEPPER TO TASTE
  JUICE OF 1 LEMON

DIRECTIONS

1. Toss all ingredients together in a large bowl until the lemon juice has coated the leaves so the herbs are well combined.
2. Serve.

BEETS, **CARROTS,** AND **RADISH** WITH **ARUGULA**

This beautiful salad boasts myriad colors, crunchy root vegetables, and just the right hint of sweet apricots.

INGREDIENTS

- **6** CUPS ARUGULA
- **3** LARGE BEETS, SLICED INTO JULIENNED PIECES
- **3** LARGE CARROTS, HEIRLOOM AND MULTI-COLORED IF POSSIBLE, JULIENNED
- A HANDFUL OF RADISHES, CUT INTO THIN ROUND SLICES
- **1** TABLESPOON ORGANIC MUSTARD
- JUICE OF 1 LEMON
- **2** TEASPOONS APPLE CIDER VINEGAR
- A SPLASH OF COLD-PRESSED OIL
- SALT AND PEPPER TO TASTE
- **1/4** CUP DRIED APRICOTS, FINELY CHOPPED

DIRECTIONS

1. Arrange the vegetables on a bed of arugula.
2. Mix the mustard, lemon juice, apple cider vinegar and oil with the salt to taste and drizzle over everything.
3. Garnish with a sprinkling of fresh or dried parsley and the chopped apricots.

HERB**COLESLAW**

This coleslaw is a classic.

INGREDIENTS

1 HEAD CABBAGE, (RED, GREEN, OR NAPA), IF THEY'RE SMALL USE 2 HEADS
1/2 CUP MIXED HERBS (CILANTRO & CHIVES, ROSEMARY & THYME, DILL & CARAWAY, OREGANO & PARSLEY), CHOPPED
SPLASH OF COLD PRESSED OIL
1/4 CUP APPLE CIDER VINEGAR
2 TABLESPOONS RAW HONEY OR AGAVE
1 TABLESPOON SEA SALT

DIRECTIONS

1. Toss all ingredients together in a large bowl until well coated, and cover in the refrigerator for a minimum of 1 hour and overnight if possible.

HERBANDENDIVE SHAVEDSALAD

Pretty and delicate.

INGREDIENTS

1/4 CUP "SOUR CREAM" (RECIPE FOUND IN RAW FOOD, FAST FOOD)
1 TABLESPOON FRESH LIME JUICE
1 TEASPOON LIME ZEST
2 CUPS PARSLEY LEAVES, FRESH
1 CUP FRESH BASIL LEAVES
1 CUP SHREDDED CHIVES
1/2 CUP MINT LEAVES
1/4 CUP FRESH TARRAGON LEAVES
2 ENDIVES, WITH THE END SLICED OFF, AND THE LEAVES SLICED HORIZONTALLY OR SLIGHTLY DIAGONALLY INTO SHARDS
SEA SALT AND PEPPER TO TASTE

SOUR CREAM

1 CUP SHREDDED AND UNSWEETENED COCONUT FLAKES
2 TABLESPOONS NUTRITIONAL YEAST
2 TABLESPOONS LIME JUICE
1 TABLESPOON LEMON JUICE
1 HEAPING TABLESPOON CHICKPEA (OR THE MELLOW WHITE) MISO
A GENEROUS PINCH OF SEA SALT
JUST ENOUGH WATER TO BLEND INTO A CREAMY SAUCE

Blend until smooth.

DIRECTIONS

1. In the bottom of a large bowl, combine the "sour cream" with lime juice and zest, sea salt and pepper.
2. Mix the herbs with the endive pieces into the dressing and toss well to coat, but not saturate the salad.
3. Garnish with chive or sage blossoms.
4. Serve.

CHIVE & SAGE SALT

This salt marinade is great rubbed on vegetables—especially zucchini that still has a "raw" taste. Use on greens and even in soups. Feel free to vary the herbs used and try different colored salts like pink or black Himalayan.

INGREDIENTS

1 TABLESPOON COLD PRESSED OIL
1 HANDFUL CRUSHED SAGE LEAVES
1 CUP FINELY MINCED CHIVES
2 TABLESPOONS COARSE SEA SALT

DIRECTIONS

1. Crush everything together in a mortar and pestle until well combined and keep in the refrigerator for a week.

MESCLUN, SUNGOLD AND KALAMATA OLIVE MASH

This is a mash. So mash it all up. Go ahead, get messy.

INGREDIENTS
1 AVOCADO, PITTED AND SLICED
1 BUNCH FRESH BASIL, RIPPED OR SHREDDED INTO PIECES
1 HANDFUL OF SUNGOLD TOMATOES PER PERSON
1/4 CUP KALAMATA OLIVES, PITTED AND SMASHED UP A BIT (THE FUN PART!)
1 LARGE HANDFUL OF MESCLUN (MIXED GREENS) PER PERSON

DIRECTIONS
1. Take the avocado, shredded basil, sungold tomatoes, kalamata olives (make sure the pits are gone!) and mash them in your hands for a few seconds, until not totally smashed, but enough to release the yummy flavors and make it look a bit messy. This really couldn't be any more fun.
2. Toss (again with your hands) with mixed greens in one large bowl and let everyone dig in, or do it as individual servings.
3. Serve and enjoy!

HEIRLOOM**TOMATO**SALAD

Classically pretty and flavorful when the tomatoes are fruiting like crazy.

INGREDIENTS

- **2** POUNDS HEIRLOOM TOMATOES, WITH THE ROUGH CORE TAKEN OUT AND SLICED INTO ROUNDS 1/4" THICK
- COARSE SEA SALT
- OPTIONAL COLD PRESSED OIL FOR DRIZZLING OVER
- **1** BUNCH FRESH BASIL, ROUGHLY CHOPPED

DIRECTIONS

1. Arrange slices on a platter, sprinkle with salt and basil.
2. Serve.

SUNGOLDS AND GREEN BEANS TOSSED WITH HERBS

Optimally, let all ingredients sit for a few hours or until the green beans are marinated. But it's fine to eat this immediately as well.

INGREDIENTS

1 LARGE HANDFUL OF FRESH GREEN BEANS, PER PERSON, ENDS DISCARDED AND SNAPPED INTO 1" PIECES
2 CUPS SUNGOLDS, HALVED
1 TABLESPOON ORGANIC (AND WITHOUT ADDITIVES) DIJON MUSTARD
1 TABLESPOON APPLE CIDER VINEGAR
   COLD-PRESSED OLIVE OIL (OPTIONAL)
   SEA SALT AND FRESH BLACK PEPPER TO TASTE
   A FEW SPRIGS OF FRESH TARRAGON
1 TABLESPOON MINCED CHIVES
   A FEW SPRIGS OF FRESH THYME

DIRECTIONS

1. Combine all ingredients in a bowl or as individual servings.
2. Serve.

CUCUMBER, RADISH AND SUNGOLD SALSA WITH MINT

A very summery recipe!

INGREDIENTS

4 CUCUMBERS, PEELED AND SLICED
1 HEAPING CUP RADISHES, WASHED AND SLICED
2 GIANT HANDFULS SUNGOLDS, HALVED
1 RED ONION, PEELED AND SLICED THINLY INTO ROUNDS
A FEW SPRIGS OF FRESH MINT, ROLLED TOGETHER AND SLICED INTO CHIFFONADE PIECES

FOR THE DRESSING

1 TABLESPOON APPLE CIDER VINEGAR
1 TABLESPOON RAW HONEY OR AGAVE
1 CLOVE OF GARLIC, PEELED AND MINCED
A PINCH OF SEA SALT
FRESH GROUND PEPPER TO TASTE

DIRECTIONS

1. In a jar with a glass lid shake until well mixed.
2. Dress the sliced vegetables, garnishing with shredded mint leaves.

TOMATO AND FENNEL PLATE

Simple as can be, elegant and summery . . . use heirloom tomatoes of all colors and sizes for a beautiful presentation.

INGREDIENTS

- 2 FENNEL BULBS, GREEN FEATHERY LEAVES TRIMMED, TOUGH OUTSIDE LAYER PEELED AWAY, COARSELY SLICED
- 3 LARGE TOMATOES, MIXED HEIRLOOMS ARE BEST
- 1 CUP SUNGOLD TOMATOES (OR CHERRY), HALVED
- JUICE OF 2 LEMONS
- 1 GENEROUS SPLASH OF BALSAMIC OR RAW APPLE CIDER VINEGAR
- COARSE SEA SALT AND FRESH BLACK PEPPER TO TASTE
- A SPRINKLE OF CHILI POWDER

DIRECTIONS

1. Slice the fennel bulbs after peeling away the outer rough skin (save a few of the feathery tops for a lovely anise garnish).
2. Slice the tomatoes.
3. Arrange the slices on one large serving platter or individual plates in whatever pattern you like.
4. Add handfuls of the halved sungolds (or cherry tomatoes).
5. Add the lemon juice and splash of vinegar.
6. Sprinkle with the coarse sea salt and black pepper and optional chili powder.
7. Serve and enjoy!

AVOCADO**CORN**RELISH

Perfect with any mix of greens, or served alone as a side.

INGREDIENTS

2 AVOCADOS, PEELED AND DICED
1 EAR OF FRESH CORN
1/2 OF A RED ONION, PEELED AND FINELY DICED
1 SMALL JALAPENO, SEEDED AND MINCED
   JUICE OF 1 LIME
   A SPLASH OF COLD PRESSED OIL
   SEASON WITH SEA SALT AND PEPPER

DIRECTIONS

1. Mix the avocado pieces with the fresh corn, onion, jalapeno.
2. Dress with lime juice and the splash of oil.
3. Season to taste and keep chilled until serving.

SWEET CHIPOTLE MARINATED MUSHROOM STEAK OVER MIXED GREENS

This recipe is meaty and flavorful. Adjust the spice to your liking. This makes a wonderful meal, and the longer it sits, the better it gets.

INGREDIENTS

JUICE OF ONE ORANGE
1 CHIPOTLE PEPPER, DRIED AND SOAKED IN WATER TO RECONSTITUTE
1 HEAPING TABLESPOON ABODO
1-2 PORTOBELLO MUSHROOMS PER PERSON

OR MAKE YOUR OWN ADOBO SEASONING:

4 CLOVES GARLIC
1 TEASPOON DRIED OREGANO
1 TEASPOON PEPPERCORNS
1/2 TEASPOON PAPRIKA
1 TEASPOON SALT

DIRECTIONS

1. Grind all the ingredients together in a mortar and pestle to make a paste.

INGREDIENTS

1 CLOVE GARLIC, PEELED AND CHOPPED
1 TABLESPOON COLD PRESSED OIL (YOUR CHOICE) OR 1 TABLESPOON HEMP SEED BUTTER

DIRECTIONS

1. Puree ingredients until smooth and soak portobello mushroom "steaks" (sliced pieces, just cut diagonally

through each cap, creating "slabs") in a container or wrapped in foil for as long as possible, but it can be as little as fifteen minutes if you're really pressed for time.

2. Serve several of the "slabs" after they've been marinating (overnight is best), over mixed greens, with a heaping spoonful or two of avocado corn relish.

AVOCADO AND ONION SLICES

Sweet, creamy, and addictive, with just the right addition of crunch and saltiness. The vegetables pair really well with the chipotle marinated salad, too.

INGREDIENTS
1 SWEET WHITE ONION, SLICED INTO ROUNDS AND THEN IN HALVES
2 AVOCADOS, PEELED, PITTED AND SLICED INTO PIECES
BLACK PEPPER, LEMON JUICE AND SPRINKLES OF COARSE SEA SALT.

DIRECTIONS
1. Arrange all slices on a plate and season with salt before serving.

TOMATO **COULIS** OVER **A** BED **OF** MESCLUN

Like so many French terms, coulis is just a fancy way of saying a thick, pureed sauce! Enjoy it here with a classic pairing: tomatoes and basil.

INGREDIENTS

- **6** HUGE HEIRLOOM TOMATOES, CUT INTO CHUNKS
- **1/2** CUP SUN-DRIED TOMATOES (IF BRITTLE, RECONSTITUTE IN WATER FOR 1/2 HOUR TO 2 HOURS)
- **1** CLOVE GARLIC, PEELED AND MINCED
- A SPLASH OF COLD PRESSED OIL (YOUR CHOICE)
- A HANDFUL FRESH BASIL LEAVES, ROUGHLY CHOPPED
- **1** TEASPOON CRUSHED RED PEPPER FLAKES
- COARSE SEA SALT AND FRESH BLACK PEPPER

DIRECTIONS

1. Puree tomatoes (fresh and sun-dried) with all ingredients except pepper, adding salt to taste, until fairly well-blended.
2. Season with black pepper and keep in refrigerator until ready to use.

SCARLETT O'HARA BOWL

Bold and passionate. A new sort of classic that has all the spunk and raciness of the heroine I named it for!

INGREDIENTS
- **2** RIPE PERSIMMONS, CHOPPED INTO PIECES (A NOTE: THE MORE RIPE AND ROTTEN LOOKING THEY ARE, THE MORE SWEET AND DELICIOUS!)
- **1** HANDFUL GOJI BERRIES
- THE SEEDS FROM ONE POMEGRANATE
- **1** RED PEPPER, SEEDED AND SLICED
- JUICE OF 1 LEMON
- **1** TABLESPOON APPLE CIDER VINEGAR
- SEA SALT AND PEPPER TO TASTE

DIRECTIONS
1. Mash together until well mixed, the persimmons, goji berries, pomegranate seeds, red pepper, lemon juice and vinegar.
2. Season with salt and pepper before serving.

EARTH AND SEA (SALAD)

The perfect blend of the two most nourishing things for our bodies (and our souls): sea and land vegetables. Sweet, salty and flavorful, with a grounding quality.

INGREDIENTS

1 CUP DRIED SEAWEED (ARAME, HIJIKI, WAKAME, ETC.)
1 RED ONION, PEELED AND DICED
1 LARGE BUNCH OF KALE
1 BUNCH SMALL HEIRLOOM CARROTS (IF YOU CAN FIND THE PURPLE AND YELLOW USE THOSE)
1 TABLESPOON COLD PRESSED OIL (HEMP, AVOCADO, OLIVE OR FLAX)
1 TABLESPOON APPLE CIDER VINEGAR
1 TEASPOON RAW HONEY OR AGAVE
A HANDFUL OF CHOPPED RAW ALMONDS

DIRECTIONS

1. Soak the seaweed in water until reconstituted, just a few minutes.
2. Drain and mix with diced onion, oil, sweetener, apple cider vinegar, preferably by hand, massaging for a few minutes, being grateful for your food, humming a song, having a great conversation...
3. Add the chopped almonds and serve.

ORANGE **AND** WHITE **SALAD**

Two colors you wouldn't necessarily put together in a salad, but it looks absolutely stunning as a starter for a dinner party: a little retro and entirely delicious.

INGREDIENTS

- **1** JICAMA, PEELED AND JULIENNED
- **1** ORANGE, SEGMENTED, PUT BACK TOGETHER AND SLICED DOWN AS IF MAKING ROUNDS
- **1** TEASPOON PAPRIKA
- JUICE OF 1 LIME
- SEA SALT TO TASTE
- PARSLEY GARNISH

DIRECTIONS

1. Mix all ingredients in a bowl or as individual servings.
2. Serve with parsley garnishes.

WHITE AND BLACK

This seems like it should be served at the San Francisco Black and White Ball or a black-tie wedding. But it's equally delicious at home as a crunchy, salty dinner you can pick at with your fingers!

INGREDIENTS

1/2 CAULIFLOWER HEAD, CUT INTO FLORETS, HALF LEFT WHOLE AND HALF CRUMBLED INTO SMALL PIECES

1 CUP KALAMATA OLIVES, SUN-DRIED, PITTED AND HALVED

SALT AND PEPPER TO TASTE

DIRECTIONS

1. Mix all ingredients and let marinate in the olive juice for a bit or serve immediately.

CUCUMBERS AND COCONUT CREAM

Perfect for a hot afternoon, or for a garden tea party, these slices are very elegant and summery.

INGREDIENTS

3 CUCUMBERS, PEELED AND SLICED INTO ROUNDS (FOR AN EXTRA FANCY AND STRIPED PRESENTATION, LEAVE STRIPS OF THE PEELING ON- BUT ONLY IF USING ORGANIC!)

CREAM

MEAT OF YOUNG THAI COCONUT

JUICE OF 1 LEMON

1 TEASPOON RAW HONEY OR AGAVE (OPTIONAL, AS IT SHOULD BE AS SOUR AS POSSIBLE LIKE A LIGHT YOGURT SAUCE)

FRESH GROUND PEPPER

DIRECTIONS

1. Slice cucumbers.
2. Add 1 tablespoon sea salt (sprinkled over the tops) and leave to sit (marinate) while making the sauce.
3. Blend together the coconut meat, lemon juice, sweetener (if using) until creamy.
4. Arrange the cucumber rounds on one plate (or individual plates if you'd prefer) if they're not already there.
5. Drizzle the sauce over the cucumber rounds and garnish with black pepper and sprigs of dill, just before serving.

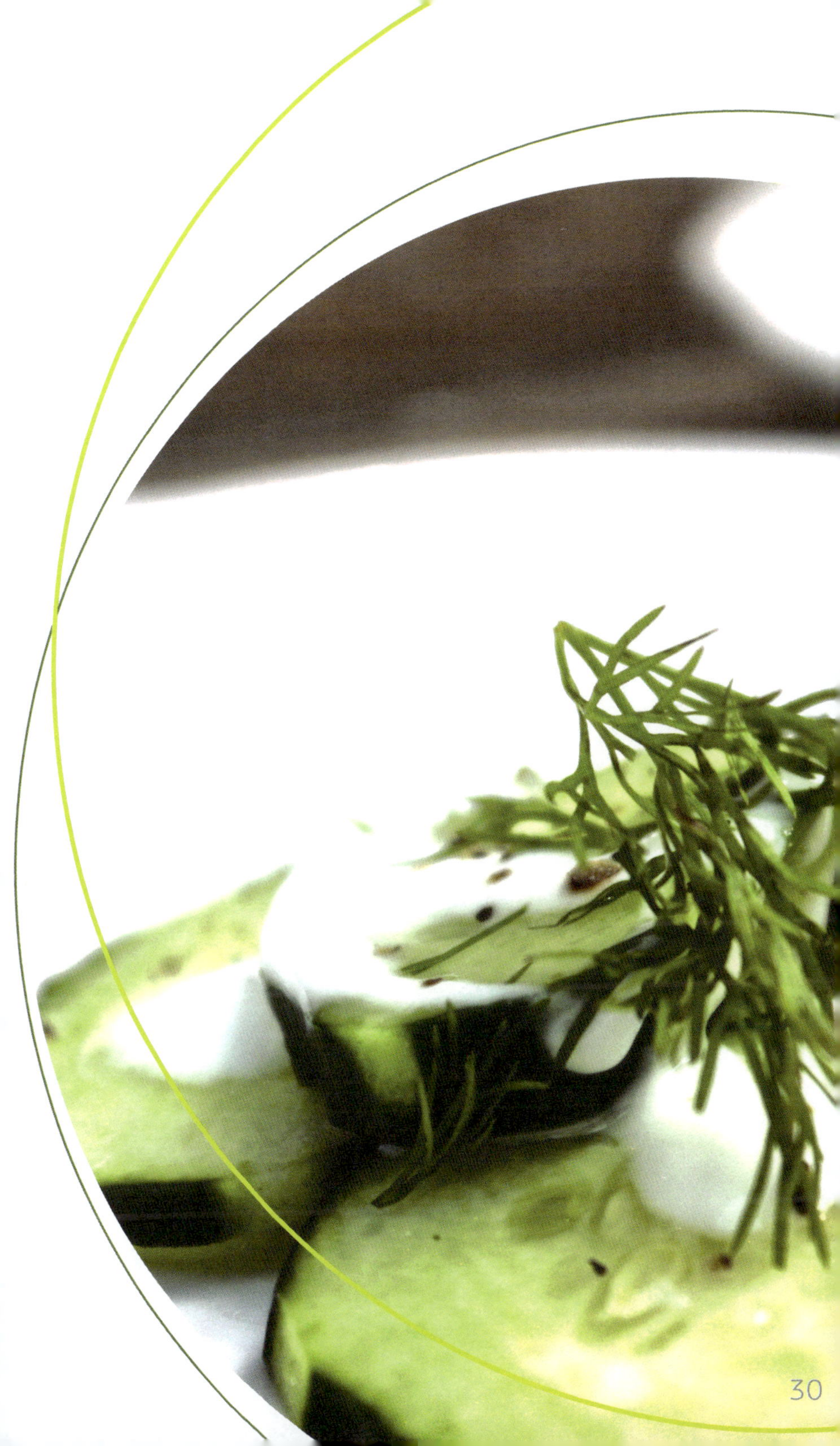

AUTUMN AND WINTER SALADS

DRAGONSLAW

A personal favorite for me. Enter the Dragon. Powerful!

INGREDIENTS

1 HEAD CABBAGE, SHREDDED
2 CARROTS, GRATED
1 RED ONION, PEELED AND MINCED
    A FEW SPRIGS OF FRESH DILL, CHOPPED
2 TABLESPOONS APPLE CIDER VINEGAR
1 TABLESPOON UMEBOSHI PLUM VINEGAR
1 TABLESPOON COLD PRESSED OIL
1 TABLESPOON RAW HONEY OR AGAVE
    SEA SALT AND FRESH BLACK PEPPER TO TASTE

DIRECTIONS

1. Combine well in a bowl and let stand in the refrigerator for a few hours (at least 1 hour) before serving OR blend all in food processor- pulse until crumbled, dress and serve.

MARINATED CELERY

Adapted from Farmer John's Cookbook: The Real Dirt on Vegetables, which was adapted from The Modern Art of Chinese Cooking. Proof that there's nothing new under the sun. We all just add our own flavors and variations, making the world a cacophony of shared taste!

INGREDIENTS

- 1 HEAD OF CELERY, CUT INTO 2" PIECES (OR SMALLER IF YOU WANT MORE OF A SALSA DISH)
- 1 GIANT TABLESPOON RAW HONEY OR AGAVE
- 1 TEASPOON COARSE SEA SALT
- 2 TABLESPOONS BRAGG'S AMINO ACIDS OR NAMA SHOYU
- 1 TABLESPOON COLD PRESSED OIL
- 1 TABLESPOON RED WINE VINEGAR
- 1 TABLESPOON UMEBOSHI PLUM VINEGAR
- 1 LARGE GARLIC CLOVE, PEELED AND MINCED (A GARLIC PRESS WORKS BEST)
- 2 TABLESPOON NUTRITIONAL YEAST
- 1 TEASPOON APPLE CIDER VINEGAR

DIRECTIONS

1. Combine the celery, raw honey and sea salt in a shallow baking dish or large bowl with your hands and let it marinate for just under an hour.
2. In a glass jar with a lid, shake up the rest of the ingredients until well combined.
3. When the celery has been sitting for almost an hour, put in a strainer and rinse with water, removing the honey and salt
4. Put the celery in a bowl or container and cover/mix well with the dressing.
5. Store in the refrigerator for 4 hours or up to 1 week, stirring occasionally.

FRENCH**BISTRO** **REMOULADE**

Ooh la la.

INGREDIENTS

- **1/2** A HEAD OF CELERIAC, WITH THE OUTER ROUGH SKIN AND KNOBS REMOVED AND CUT INTO MATCHSTICK PIECES
- JUICE OF 1 LEMON
- **2** TABLESPOONS DIJON MUSTARD
- CAPERS (OPTIONAL, BUT THEY REALLY DO ADD A NECESSARY COMPONENT TO THE FLAVOR; YOU CAN FIND THEM IN HEALTH FOOD STORES WITHOUT ANY ADDITIVES)
- HERBES DE PROVENCE (TO MAKE YOUR OWN: 2 TABLESPOONS THYME, 2 TABLESPOONS SAVORY OR OREGANO, 2 TABLESPOONS LAVENDER, 1 TEASPOON BASIL, 1 TEASPOON SAGE, 1 TEASPOON CRUSHED ROSEMARY, BLENDED TOGETHER AND STORED IN AIRTIGHT CONTAINER)
- SEA SALT
- FRESH BLACK PEPPER
- **2** TABLESPOON NUTRITIONAL YEAST
- **1** TEASPOON APPLE CIDER VINEGAR

DIRECTIONS

1. Start by mixing a creamy "mayo" sauce in the bottom of a large bowl with 2 tablespoons nutritional yeast, 1 teaspoon apple cider vinegar and just enough water to make it into a liquid.
2. Add the julienned celeriac, lemon juice, mustard and herbes de provence.
3. Toss and stand for an hour or more.
4. Add the capers and serve with sea salt and black pepper to taste.

APPLE PARSNIP AUTUMN SALAD

This salad is delightfully crunchy and sweet, and can be made quickly by pulsing the apples and parsnips in a food processor with the other ingredients added or dressed later.

INGREDIENTS
2 APPLES, ANY VARIETY IN SEASON, SHREDDED OR JULIENNED
2 PARSNIPS, GRATED OR JULIENNED
1 TEASPOON CINNAMON
1 QUICK SPLASH OF COLD-PRESSED OLIVE OIL
SEA SALT AND BLACK PEPPER TO TASTE

DIRECTIONS
1. Serve over mixed greens with a dash of nutmeg to garnish.

SPICY**SWEET**SLAW

This makes enough to keep extra in the fridge, so it continues to marinate and just keep getting more delicious!

INGREDIENTS
1 NAPA CABBAGE, BASE OF THE STEM AND TOUGH INNER LEAVES DISCARDED
1 CUP RAISINS
3 LARGE CARROTS, SHREDDED
3 APPLES, WHATEVER VARIETY IS IN SEASON, 2 CORED AND SHREDDED AND 1 CORED AND CHOPPED INTO 1" PIECES

DRESSING
1/2 CUP APPLE CIDER VINEGAR
1/4 CUP HONEY
2 TABLESPOONS MUSTARD
1 JALAPENO, SEEDED
1 TABLESPOON COARSE SEA SALT
1 TEASPOON GROUND PEPPER
2 TABLESPOONS COLD PRESSED OIL- OPTIONAL

DIRECTIONS
1. Soak everything, tossed together and shredded well, for at least 15 minutes.
2. Toss with dressing before serving. The longer it marinates, the more delicious it will be!

NORDIC**WINTER**SALAD

If you've stored some root vegetables, this will be heavenly and a taste of local freshness in the depths of winter!

INGREDIENTS
- **1** SMALL RUTABAGA, GRATED
- **2** CARROTS, JULIENNED INTO THIN MATCHSTICKS
- **1** MEDIUM BEET, GRATED
- **1** LARGE HANDFUL OF DATES (OR APRICOTS), FINELY CHOPPED
- **2** RIPE APRICOTS, PITTED
- **1** CLOVE GARLIC (OR SHALLOT), PEELED AND MINCED
- GENEROUS SPLASH OF LEMON JUICE
- A GENEROUS PINCH EACH: CARAWAY SEEDS, THYME, AND ALLSPICE
- BLACK PEPPER AND SEA SALT TO TASTE

DIRECTIONS
1. Combine the sliced vegetables and chopped dried fruit with the apricot, mashed up well.
2. Add a splash of lemon juice, the minced garlic (or shallot), and a generous pinch of each of the seasonings.
3. Season with sea salt and fresh ground black pepper to taste and serve as is or over a bed of mixed greens.

MISTAKEN **IDENTITY** SALAD

Jerusalem artichokes (or sunchokes) are neither from Jerusalem nor are they actual artichokes.

But there's no mistaking the deliciousness of this salad.

INGREDIENTS

- **1** HANDFUL SUNCHOKES PER SERVING (MOST HANDS CAN PICK UP 3-4 FOR MORE OF AN IDEA!), PEELED AND FINELY DICED
- ROUGHLY 1 HANDFUL MIXED GREENS PER PERSON
- **1** CUP RAISINS
- **1** CLOVE GARLIC, PEELED AND MINCED
- **1** TABLESPOON SEA SALT
- **2** TABLESPOONS CHERVIL LEAVES (FRESH OR DRIED)
- **1** TABLESPOON APPLE CIDER VINEGAR
- **2** LARGE CARROTS, PEELED AND FINELY DICED (OR SHREDDED)
- **3** CUPS SPROUTS (ANY KIND, OR A MIXTURE)
- JUICE OF 1 FRESH LEMON
- **1** TABLESPOON RAW HONEY OR MAPLE SYRUP (ADJUSTING TO TASTE)

DIRECTIONS

1. In a large bowl, mix together the lemon juice, apple cider vinegar, chervil, sea salt, minced garlic, and sweetener until well combined.
2. Add the artichokes, carrots, raisins, and sprouts until thoroughly coated and let sit for as long as you can before serving to let the flavors fully settle in.
3. Toss with mixed greens and enjoy!

INGREDIENTS

1 HEAD CAULIFLOWER, STEM AND LEAVES DISCARDED, FLORETS FINELY DICED
2 MEDIUM SWEET POTATOES, SCRUBBED AND FINELY DICED (NO NEED TO PEEL)
3 MEDIUM TOMATOES, SEEDED AND COARSELY CHOPPED

DIRECTIONS

1. Mix above ingredients together with:

1 TABLESPOON BRAGGS OR NAMA SHOYU
1 TABLESPOON RAW HONEY (OR AGAVE OR MAPLE SYRUP)
1 KNOB OF GINGER, PEELED AND JUICED IN A HANDHELD GARLIC PRESS
1 TABLESPOON APPLE CIDER VINEGAR
1 TEASPOON DRIED BASIL LEAVES AND PINK HIMALAYAN SALT OR COARSE SEA SALT, TO TASTE

2. Left as long as possible to marinate, but it can be served immediately if needed.

SWEET POTATO, CAULIFLOWER & TOMATO SALAD

An unlikely mix, but so delicious, and so easy. Perfect over a bed of greens or lettuce leaves.

MARINATED RAW BEET SALAD WITH BASIL

Make this as far ahead of time as possible for optimal flavor.

INGREDIENTS

- 4 BEETS, PEELED AND GRATED
- 1/4 CUP COLD PRESSED OLIVE OIL
- 3 TABLESPOONS RAW APPLE CIDER VINEGAR
- 1 SHALLOT, PEELED AND FINELY DICED
- 1 TEASPOON ORGANIC DIJON OR STONE-GROUND MUSTARD (NO SUGAR ADDED)
- 1 CLOVE GARLIC, PEELED AND FINELY MINCED (A GARLIC PRESS WORKS BEST OR REALLY MASTICATE IT WITH A CHOPPING KNIFE)
- 2 TABLESPOONS FRESH DILL TO GARNISH, CHOPPED COARSE SEA SALT AND FRESH BLACK PEPPER, TO TASTE

DIRECTIONS

1. Grate the beets into a large bowl.
2. In a mason (or any) jar with a lid, combine the oil, vinegar, shallot, mustard and garlic, and shake until well combined.
3. Add the dressing to the bowl of beets, and mix until completely covered.
4. Season with salt and pepper and set in the fridge to marinate for as long as possible (at least 1 hour).
5. Before serving, garnish with fresh dill.

SWEET BABY BRUSSELS BLEND

Little baby brussels sprouts are not the tasteless, overcooked variety you might have tramatizing flashbacks about. These are tender and bursting with flavor, and paired with the honey and vinegar, they're elevated to a delightful new level. Create new brussels sprout memories with this yummy salad!

INGREDIENTS

- BRUSSELS SPROUTS, ROUGHLY CHOPPED TO EQUAL ABOUT 2 CUPS
- **2** CARROTS, GRATED
- **1/2** SWEET ONION (WALLA WALLA, VIDALIA, ETC.)
- **1** HANDFUL DRIED DATES, CHOPPED
- **2** TABLESPOONS APPLE CIDER VINEGAR
- **1** TABLESPOON RAW HONEY OR AGAVE
- A GENEROUS SPLASH OF BALSAMIC VINEGAR
- A TINY DASH OF NUTMEG AND PAPRIKA
- SEA SALT
- BLACK PEPPER

DIRECTIONS

1. Combine well and let sit in the refrigerator for several hours (overnight if possible) before serving.

CARROT AND POPPY SEED SALAD WITH CREAM SAUCE

Simple, delicious, and the poppy seeds make for a nice surprise. Extra cream sauce can be kept in the fridge!

INGREDIENTS

- **2** CARROTS, MATCHSTICK SLICED
- **2** SMALL CUCUMBERS, MATCHSTICK SLICED
- **1** FENNEL BULB, SLICED THINLY INTO MATCHSTICKS
- BALSAMIC VINEGAR, SPRINKLED OVER VEGGIES
- SEA SALT
- **2** TABLESPOONS POPPY SEEDS, SPRINKLED LIBERALLY OVER EVERYTHING ONCE DRESSED
- **1** YOUNG THAI COCONUT, MEAT AND WATER
- **2** TABLESPOONS LEMON JUICE
- SEA SALT TO TASTE

DIRECTIONS

1. Blend coconut meat with lemon juice and sea salt in the blender until creamy.
2. Mix the carrots, cucumbers, and fennel slices together in a large bowl.
3. Put a spoonful of the coconut yogurt on top of each serving, followed by a splash of balsamic vinegar and a liberal sprinkling of poppy seeds.

GINGERED DRAGON BOWL OF BROCCOLI

A sweet, spicy dish that's reminiscent of some of the more exciting entrees at Szechuan restaurants. Dig in—but keep some water handy!

FOR THE BOWL:
1 HEAD OF BROCCOLI, CUT INTO LITTLE FLORETS
1 TABLESPOON GOJI BERRIES
1 TABLESPOON MAPLE SYRUP
2 TABLESPOONS NAMA SHOYU OR BRAGG'S
1 TABLESPOON APPLE CIDER VINEGAR

FOR THE MEATBALLS:
4 TABLESPOONS NUTRITIONAL YEAST
2 TABLESPOONS MESQUITE
1 TABLESPOON MAPLE SYRUP
1 TABLESPOON MACA
1 TABLESPOON HEMP SEED BUTTER
1/2 ONION, PEELED AND FINELY DICED
1/2 TEASPOON EACH: CUMIN, MARJORAM, PEPPER, NUTMEG, OREGANO, ALLSPICE, CAYENNE PEPPER, CHIPOTLE, GINGER (FRESH MINCED OR GROUND POWDER), PAPRIKA
1 TABLESPOON EACH: DRIED BASIL, THYME, SAGE

DIRECTIONS

1. Mix all ingredients together in a bowl with a spoon or your fingers.
2. When it's all combined and sticky, break off tablespoon size pieces and instead of packing firmly, just gently and quickly mash into meatballs, leaving them looking rough for a "meaty" texture.
3. Marinate the broccoli pieces (remember that the smaller the pieces, the more flavor they'll soak up) in the maple syrup,

bragg's and apple cider vinegar for several hours, overnight if possible. Massage the pieces a bit with your hands before leaving it to sit, to really get the flavors mingling together.
4. Serve over a handful of mixed greens per person or with a big sprig of fresh basil.

PESTO SALAD

Think pesto is just for pasta? Think again! This salad brings all of the taste of a pesto dinner to life, but without the starchy grains.

INGREDIENTS

- **4** CUPS ARUGULA LEAVES
- **1/2** CUP NUTRITIONAL YEAST
- **2** TABLESPOONS PINE NUTS
- **1** TABLESPOON SEA SALT
- **1** CLOVE GARLIC, PEELED AND MINCED
- ENOUGH COLD PRESSED OLIVE OIL TO DRIZZLE IN AS PROCESSING (YOU DON'T WANT TOO MUCH)

DIRECTIONS

1. Blend until combined but still a bit chunky.
2. Serve over a bed of mesclun greens and mix together until the leaves are mostly coated.
3. Add some freshly ground black pepper to taste.

DELHI CARROTS

Indian spices make these carrot ribbons beautiful and flavorful. With mixed greens, this salad is incredible and can be a lovely light lunch, or substantial dinner that kids go mad for. Kids also love to go to work with a vegetable peeler and a large bowl to make the ribbons, providing you with both amusement and kitchen aid!

INGREDIENTS

- **1** POUND DIFFERENT COLORED CARROTS, HEIRLOOM IF POSSIBLE (THERE ARE AMAZING VARIETIES AVAILABLE IN PURPLE, ORANGE AND YELLOW)

DRESSING:
1 TABLESPOON GARAM MASALA (FANTASTIC INDIAN SPICE THAT IS READILY AVAILABLE AT MOST SUPERMARKETS AND HEALTH FOOD STORES)
1 TEASPOON GROUND CUMIN
2 SHALLOTS, PEELED AND MINCED
JUICE OF ONE LEMON (OR LIME FOR FLAVOR VARIATION) WITH THE ZEST
MINCED OR GRATED GINGER (1 OR 2 KNOBS OR ROUGHLY 1 TABLESPOON)
SEA SALT, TO TASTE
COLD-PRESSED OLIVE OIL, ENOUGH TO DRIZZLE AND MAKE THE SESAME SEEDS STICK

HANDFUL OF EACH FOR GARNISH:
SESAME SEEDS
FRESH CILANTRO
FRESH MINT

DIRECTIONS
1. Shave into ribbons with peeler, leaving a few pieces in varying shapes and slices.
2. Combine with the dressing in a large bowl, mixing with hands until well covered.
3. Arrange on individual plates.
4. Garnish with cilantro, mint, paprika and sesame seeds.

MIXED BOK CHOY

Bok Choy is a delicious vegetable and highly under-used vegetable, in my opinion!

INGREDIENTS

- **1** HEAD BOK CHOY, SLICED AND CHOPPED FINELY
- **2** TABLESPOONS APPLE CIDER VINEGAR
- **1** TABLESPOON BRAGG'S AMINO ACIDS OR NAMA SHOYU
- **1** TABLESPOON CHILI POWDER
- **1** TABLESPOON RAW HONEY OR AGAVE (THE LATTER POURS A BIT EASIER BUT HONEY CAN BE MASSAGED IN WITH A BIT OF EXTRA TIME) A SPLASH OF COLD PRESSED OIL (OPTIONAL)
- **1** CUP RAW NUTS (MACADAMIA ARE ESPECIALLY DELICIOUS), CHOPPED ROUGHLY
- SEA SALT AND PEPPER TO TASTE

DIRECTIONS

1. Roughly chop and dice the bok choy, discarding the very root of the head.
2. Massage in a bowl with the apple cider vinegar, Bragg's, sweetener, chili powder, and cold pressed oil (optional).
3. When ready to serve, add the coarsely chopped nuts, sea salt and freshly ground pepper to taste.
4. Serve immediately or keep in fridge for several hours, up to several days (covered).

COURGETTE**RIBBON**SALAD

Courgette is the elegant, French name for zucchini, and this is truly an elegant salad! Kids also love to help with the slices.

INGREDIENTS

4 ZUCCHINI
1 CLOVE GARLIC, PEELED AND MINCED
   SEA SALT AND FRESH GROUND PEPPER
1 FRESH RED CHILI, FINELY DICED (OR 1 TABLESPOON DRIED CHILI FLAKES & SEEDS)
   A HANDFUL OF FRESH MINT
1 TABLESPOON COLD-PRESSED OIL (OLIVE, HEMP, FLAX, AVOCADO)
   JUICE OF 1 LEMON
2 CUPS PEAS, EITHER SHELLED OR SUGAR SNAPS, (WHOLE OR HALVED)

DIRECTIONS

1. Slice the zucchini with a mandolin or handheld vegetable peeler into long-as-possible strips that are almost transparent, alternating on all sides of the zucchini until you reach too many seeds in the middle to keep slicing.
2. Arrange on a platter.
3. Sprinkle sea salt and black pepper, chili pepper (or flakes), garlic, oil, lemon and peas.
4. Garnish with freshly torn mint leaves.

FRUIT SALADS

ENDLESS SUMMER FRUIT SALAD

These summer fruits with lemon and sweetener are absolute hot weather perfection. They'll please every palate, even super picky kids.

INGREDIENTS

1/4 CUP AGAVE OR MAPLE SYRUP OR RAW HONEY
1/4 CUP FRESH MINCED MINT OR LEMON VERBENA LEAVES
2 T LEMON OR LIME JUICE
2 CUPS HALVED GRAPES
2 PEACHES
2 NECTARINES
2 LARGE HANDFULS SLICED STRAWBERRIES
1 HANDFUL EACH RASPBERRIES AND BLACKBERRIES
2 CUPS BLUEBERRIES

DIRECTIONS

1. Mix all fruit with the juices and sweetener and crushed leaves.
2. Let sit in the fridge for a few hours or overnight to let the flavors combine.

YOUNG THAI COCONUT BOWL

Young Thai coconuts make for an unexpected—yet highly impressive—presentation in this dish.

INGREDIENTS

- **1** YOUNG THAI COCONUT PER PERSON, TOP OPENED, WATER SAVED FOR ANOTHER USE, AND MEAT SCRAPED OUT
- **1** RED PEPPER FOR EVERY TWO SERVINGS (I.E. 1/2 PEPPER PER PERSON)
- **2** MANGOES, PEELED AND SLICED INTO MATCHSTICK PIECES
- **1"** KNOB FRESH GINGER, PEELED AND MINCED (A GARLIC PRESS WORKS REALLY WELL FOR THIS)
- **1** AVOCADO, PITTED AND FINELY DICED
- **2** TABLESPOONS LIME JUICE
- MIX OF ARUGULA AND WATERCRESS, ROUGHLY 1 GIANT HANDFUL PER PERSON
- SEA SALT AND FRESH GROUND PEPPER TO TASTE

DIRECTIONS

1. Place the washed arugula and watercress in a large bowl.
2. On top of the greens, mix the coconut meat (chopped into pieces if it's a bit tough, otherwise leave in silken strands) with the red pepper, mango, avocado and minced ginger.
3. Toss with the lime juice until just barely covered.
4. Fill halved and hollowed out coconut shells for a fun and interesting serving presentation!

GREEN**TANG**SALAD*

It's so easy being green: just ask anyone who tries this deliciously tangy salad with a crunch.

INGREDIENTS

4-5 GREEN GARDEN TOMATOES, SEEDED AND DICED
2 GREEN APPLES (GRANNY SMITH)
1 LARGE ONION, PEELED AND DICED
1 GREEN PEPPER, SEEDED AND DICED
1/4 CUP APPLE CIDER VINEGAR
3 STALKS OF CELERY, CHOPPED
1 TABLESPOON RAW HONEY OR AGAVE OR MAPLE SYRUP
1 TEASPOON CORIANDER SEEDS
1 TEASPOON COARSE SEA SALT

DIRECTIONS

1. Mix all ingredients together and serve as is, like a salsa with sliced veggies, or on top of a bed of mixed greens or lettuce.

ALSO DELICIOUS AS A STUFFING FOR HALVED TOMATOES, PEPPERS OR STEMMED MUSHROOM CAPS.

SWEET CELERIAC (SLAW)

You wouldn't imagine celeriac to taste so sweet and delightful. But don't you love being surprised?

INGREDIENTS

2 APPLES, WHICHEVER VARIETY YOU LIKE, CORED AND SLICED INTO THIN PIECES

1 MEDIUM CELERIAC, ROUGH OUTSIDE CUT OFF, SLICED AND JULIENNED THINLY

RAW NUTS, SUCH AS WALNUTS, ALMONDS, MACADAMIA OR PECANS (OPTIONAL)

JUICE OF 1 LEMON

2 TABLESPOONS NUTRITIONAL YEAST,

1 TABLESPOON RAW HONEY OR AGAVE

1 TABLESPOON DIJON MUSTARD

1 TABLESPOON APPLE CIDER VINEGAR

1 TEASPOON SEA SALT (OR TO TASTE)

WATER TO THIN IF NEEDED

FRESH BLACK PEPPER

DIRECTIONS

1. Toss well in large bowl and let sit in refrigerator for as long as possible, over night if possible to fully marinate and combine.

SHADES**OF**RED**AND**PINK

Simple, beautiful, perfect for any occasion and fun for kids to help prepare, although good luck keeping them from eating most of it as it's being made!

INGREDIENTS
1/2 WATERMELON, CUT INTO 1" PIECES, SEEDED
3 RED TOMATOES
2 TABLESPOONS BALSAMIC VINEGAR
1/2 BUNCH FRESH BASIL LEAVES, SHREDDED

DIRECTIONS
1. Mix all ingredients together until just covered with balsamic vinegar and either chill in the fridge for a few hours or serve immediately.

MINTED BASIL & CITRUS MELON

Gorgeous and perfect for a hot summer day. This works as a dinner party starter, a light lunch or even a fuss-free dessert.

INGREDIENTS

- JUICE OF 1 LIME
- **1** TABLESPOON APPLE CIDER VINEGAR
- GRATED LEMON ZEST OF 1 LIME
- **1** BUNCH FRESH MINT, SHREDDED
- **1** BUNCH FRESH LEMON VERBENA, SHREDDED
- **4** FRESH BASIL LEAVES, SHREDDED
- **1** MEDIUM MELON (CANTALOUPE IS HEAVENLY)
- **3** DRIED OR FRESH FIGS, QUARTERED
- **2** GREEN ONIONS, MINCED

DIRECTIONS

1. Combine lime juice, vinegar, zest until well mixed.
2. Add the thinly sliced herb leaves.
3. Arrange melon scoops on a plate.
4. Pour the dressing mixture over the fruit, season with cinnamon and fresh black pepper.

INGREDIENTS

- **2** CUPS GRAPES, HALVED
- **1** AVOCADO, PITTED AND DICED
- **4** CUPS SPINACH LEAVES
- **1** CUP FRESH CORN
- **1** SHALLOT, PEELED AND MINCED
- **1/2** CUP COARSELY CHOPPED MACADAMIA NUTS
- **2** TABLESPOONS DIJON MUSTARD
- **2** TABLESPOONS APPLE CIDER VINEGAR
- **1** TEASPOON GROUND CORIANDER

DIRECTIONS

1. In a large bowl, combine the spinach leaves with the corn, halved grapes, and chopped nuts.
2. Whisk the minced shallots, dijon mustard, apple cider vinegar and coriander until well combined and add to the rest of the ingredients.
3. Just barely toss the avocado pieces with everything and serve.

PURPLE, GREEN AND YELLOW SALAD

Full of antioxidants, selenium, vitamin E and lutein, so it's like a medicinal boost for your body as well as a flavor explosion for your tastebuds!

AVOCADO **AND** GRAPEFRUIT WITH PEPITAS **AND** COCONUT

Avocado and grapefruit are famous flavor companions, but the pepitas and coconut give this salad a snappy crunch and loads of added nutrition.

INGREDIENTS

1 AVOCADO, PITTED AND DICED
2 GRAPEFRUITS, PEELED AND CUT INTO SECTIONS
1 SMALL RED ONION, PEELED AND DICED
2 TABLESPOONS RAW HONEY OR AGAVE
2 TABLESPOONS LIME JUICE
1/4 CUP RAW PEPITAS (PUMPKIN SEEDS)
1/4 CUP SHREDDED COCONUT FLAKES
SEVERAL BUNCHES OF ARUGULA

DIRECTIONS

1. Whisk together the lime juice and honey or agave.
2. Arrange the grapefruit, onion and avocado on top of the arugula leaves for each individual serving.
3. Garnish with sprinkles of pepitas and shredded coconut and a touch of chili powder.

RUBIES AND EMERALDS
(SPINACH AND STRAWBERRY SALAD)

Makes for a stunning presentation.

INGREDIENTS

- **6** CUPS SPINACH
- **3** CUPS STRAWBERRIES
- **1"** KNOB FRESH GINGER, PEELED AND MINCED (IN A GARLIC PRESS IS THE BEST WAY)
- **1** TABLESPOON COLD-PRESSED OIL
- **1** TABLESPOON BALSAMIC OR APPLE CIDER VINEGAR
- **1** TABLESPOON AGAVE NECTAR
- **1** TEASPOON CHILI POWDER
- A PINCH OF CAYENNE (1/4-1 TEASPOON DEPENDING ON YOUR PREFERENCE)
- SALT AND PEPPER

DIRECTIONS

1. Slice the strawberries and add to a large bowl of spinach leaves.
2. In a small bowl (or mason jar with a lid) mix (or shake) the minced ginger, oil, vinegar, agave, chili powder, cayenne, salt and pepper (to taste).
3. Dress the spinach and strawberries, mixing until thoroughly coated and serve.

BALSAMIC STRAWBERRIES AND BRUNOST WITH ARUGULA

Brunost is Norwegian for brown cheese, and the chevre-like "cheese" for this salad has the addition of fermented soy spread and sauce, so it has a definite brown tinge. The saltiness combines perfectly with the tangy vinegar, sweet strawberries, and herbs.

FOR THE SALAD

1 LARGE HANDFUL OF ARUGULA PER SERVING
1 HANDFUL OF STRAWBERRIES PER SERVING, HALVED
2 TABLESPOONS BALSAMIC VINEGAR
1/2 BUNCH BASIL LEAVES, SNIPPED OR SHREDDED INTO PIECES
SEA SALT AND PEPPER TO GARNISH

FOR THE BRUNOST

1 TABLESPOON BRAGG'S OR NAMA SHOYU
1 TABLESPOON LEMON JUICE
2 TABLESPOONS NUTRITIONAL YEAST
1 TEASPOON MISO
1 TEASPOON DRIED BASIL

DIRECTIONS

1. In a small bowl mix together the brunost ingredients until you have a creamy "cheese".
2. In a large bowl mix the arugula with the halved strawberries, toss with the balsamic vinegar, shredded basil and a dash of salt and pepper to taste.

MORNING**GLORY**SALAD

Did you know that sweet potatoes are members of the morning glory family? They're incredibly nutritious, when they're eaten raw, they even help pull heavy metals out of our bodies. Delightful anytime of the day.

INGREDIENTS

1 SWEET POTATO, PEELED AND GRATED
2 APPLES, CORED AND JULIENNED
1/2 CUP RAW WALNUTS
2 TABLESPOONS RAW HONEY OR MAPLE SYRUP
1 TABLESPOON APPLE CIDER (OR BALSAMIC) VINEGAR
JUICE OF 1 LIME AND 1 TEASPOON OF THE ZEST
1/4 CUP COCONUT FLAKES (OR THE LARGE CHIPS)
1 TEASPOON GROUND CINNAMON
1 TEASPOON CHILI POWDER
1/2 TEASPOON GROUND GINGER
1/4 TEASPOON ALLSPICE
A DASH OF NUTMEG
A QUICK DASH OF VANILLA EXTRACT OR 1 TEASPOON VANILLA POWDER

DIRECTIONS

1. Mix all ingredients together in a large bowl. It's best if you let this salad sit for as long as possible for the flavors to marinate, but it can also be served immediately and is just as tasty.

MINTED **PEACHES,** CORN **SALSA & SMOKY** MESQUITE SAUCE **OVER** MIXED **GREENS**

Sweet, smokey and minty. Silky textures combine with beautiful crunch in the form of red and green leaves.

FOR THE MESQUITE SAUCE
1 TABLESPOON MESQUITE POWDER
2 TABLESPOONS AGAVE
1 TABLESPOON WATER (OR JUST ENOUGH TO MAKE THE SAUCE LIQUID ENOUGH TO DRIZZLE OVER THE SALAD, BUT NOT TOO WATERY
A PINCH OF SEA SALT AND A LARGER PINCH OF CHILI POWDER

1. Blend in a bowl until smooth and set aside.

FOR THE SALSA
2 CUPS FRESH CORN
   JUICE OF 1 LIME JUICE
2 TEASPOONS GROUND CUMIN
1 TEASPOON CHIPOTLE POWDER
1 HANDFUL GREEN ONIONS, FINELY DICED
1 RED BELL PEPPER, SEEDED AND FINELY DICED
1 CLOVE GARLIC, PEELED AND MINCED

1. Mix all ingredients together and set aside.

FOR THE SALAD
2 HANDFULS MESCLUN MIX FOR EACH SERVING
3 VERY RIPE PEACHES, PITTED AND SLICED
1 HEAPING TABLESPOON FRESH MINT LEAVES, RIPPED INTO PIECES

DIRECTIONS

1. Mash the peach slices up a bit with the shredded mint leaves until well combined and a bit messy looking.
2. Toss over the mixed greens.
3. Cover with salsa and mesquite sauce.
4. Serve with a dash of fresh ground pepper and smoked paprika and a few fresh mint leaves.

PART II: SOUPS

SIMPLE AND QUICK SOUPS

Simplicity and ease of preparation reigns supreme in these soup recipes. Raw ingredients means you're not waiting for soups to cook, so you can enjoy the vibrant and nourishing health benefits and all the enzymes immediately—and without burning your mouth!

A hand-held blender is often all the equipment necessary, which makes them even easier.

CREAMY COMFORT SOUPS

MARRAKESH EXPRESS

Holding this bowl in your hands, you can almost smell the Moroccan spices wafting through the open-air markets of the Red City.

INGREDIENTS
- **4** LARGE CARROTS, GRATED
- **2** AVOCADOS, PITTED
- JUICE OF 1 LIME
- **1** KNOB OF GINGER, ROUGHLY AN INCH, PRESSED INTO JUICE THROUGH GARLIC PRESS
- **1/2** TEASPOON CUMIN
- **1/2** TEASPOON CORIANDER
- **1** TEASPOON SEA SALT
- A SPRINKLE OF CAYENNE (TO YOUR SPICE PREFERENCE)
- CHOPPED CILANTRO AND BLACK PEPPER TO GARNISH

DIRECTIONS

1. In a high speed blender (or in a large bowl with a hand-held blender) mix the grated carrots, avocado, lime juice, minced ginger, cumin, coriander, and sea salt with enough water (start with 1 1/2 cups and then add more, up to 3, if necessary) to make a creamy but not too watery soup.
2. Add the cayenne, cilantro and black pepper to taste and serve.

INGREDIENTS

- 2 CUPS WATER (MAY NEED MORE AS BLENDING)
- 1 AVOCADO
- 2 CUPS FRESH OR FROZEN PEAS
- 1 TEASPOON COLD PRESSED OIL
- 1 YELLOW ONION, PEELED AND CHOPPED
- 2 CARROTS, WASHED AND GRATED
- 1 CLOVE GARLIC, PEELED AND MINCED
- 1 TABLESPOON SUN-DRIED TOMATOES, RECONSTITUTED IN WATER OR PACKED IN OIL (WITHOUT PRESERVATIVES OR SUGAR OF COURSE!)
- 1 TABLESPOON BRAGG'S AMINO ACIDS OR NAMA SHOYU
- 1 TABLESPOON FRESH ROSEMARY OR 1 TEASPOON DRIED
- 1 TEASPOON PAPRIKA
- SEA SALT AND PEPPER TO TATSTE
- A FEW SPRIGS OF FRESH PARSLEY OR ROSEMARY TO GARNISH

DIRECTIONS

1. Blend everything until smooth except the parsley and rosemary garnish.
2. Season to taste and add garnish on top.

ROSEMARY**PEA**SOUP

Reminiscent of Tuscany, with a lovely and earthy flavor.

SILKY SPINACH WITH STRANDS OF DULSE

A creamy garden soup with the added nutrition and smoky flavor of right-from-the-ocean dulse strands, deep burgundy and beautiful in the bowls.

INGREDIENTS

2 HANDFULS ORGANIC, WASHED SPINACH LEAVES
1/4 CUP ALOE (THE INNER FILLET SCRAPED OUT) OR GEL
1 KNOB OF FRESH GINGER, PEELED AND FINELY MINCED
1 TABLESPOON MIRIN (OR APPLE CIDER VINEGAR IF YOU PREFER)
1 TABLESPOON KELP POWDER
   A GENEROUS HANDFUL OF DULSE, RIPPED INTO 1" PIECES
1 TABLESPOON MISO
2 CUPS WATER

DIRECTIONS

1. Blend all ingredients except the dulse, saving the miso for the end of the blending, so it doesn't heat up. Season with additional sea salt if you want, but the kelp and miso will most likely give it enough of a salty taste.
2. Add the dulse pieces to each individual serving, and add freshly ground pepper to each bowl.

MUSHROOM**GINGER**STEW

For this stew you can use whatever mushrooms you have available, but shiitake are exceptionally good. Add some diced pieces added after blending, as they're chewy and flavorful.

INGREDIENTS

- 1 AVOCADO, PITTED
- 2 CUPS MIXED VARIETIES OF MUSHROOMS (1 CUP TO BLEND AND 1 CUP -PREFERABLY SHIITAKE- DICED AND ADDED TO EACH SERVING)
- 1 CLOVE GARLIC, PEELED AND MINCED
- 1 TABLESPOON COLD-PRESSED OIL (YOUR CHOICE AVOCADO, FLAX, OLIVE, ETC.)
- 1 TABLESPOON BRAGGS AMINO ACIDS OR NAMA SHOYU
- 1 TABLESPOON MISO
- 1 TEASPOON RAW HONEY OR AGAVE
- 2 CUPS CHOPPED RED TOMATOES
- 1 KNOB OF GINGER (ROUGHLY 1 INCH LONG) OR 1 HEAPING TABLESPOON GINGER POWDER (IF USING THE FRESH GINGER, EITHER PEEL AND FINELY MINCE OR PEEL AND SQUEEZE THROUGH A GARLIC PRESS FOR THE JUICE)
- A HANDFUL OF THIN CARROT PEELS/CURLS
- A FEW SPRIGS OF CILANTRO TO GARNISH
- SALT AND PEPPER, TO TASTE

DIRECTIONS

1. Blend 1 cup of the mushrooms with the avocado, ginger, garlic, Bragg's, miso and sweetener until creamy, adding sea salt to taste.
2. Pour into one large bowl that people can ladle from or into individual bowls. Add the diced shiitakes, chopped tomatoes, carrot curls, cilantro sprigs and pepper.
3. Serve.

MEXICAN CREAM

Mmmmm, time for a siesta? With this soup, your mouth will more likely be ready for a fiesta!!

INGREDIENTS

1 YOUNG THAI COCONUT, WATER AND MEAT
2 TABLESPOONS RAW HEMP SEED BUTTER (OR ANY RAW NUT BUTTER)
1 HEAPING TABLESPOON RAW HONEY OR AGAVE
1 CLOVE GARLIC, PEELED AND MINCED
1 MEDIUM YELLOW ONION, PEELED AND COARSELY CHOPPED
1/2 CUP WATER (OR ENOUGH TO BRING TO DESIRED CONSISTENCY WHILE BLENDING)
1 TEASPOON GROUND CINNAMON
1 POBLANO CHILE, DICED (ALWAYS ADJUST HOT PEPPER MEASUREMENTS TO YOUR DESIRED SPICE LEVELS)
1/2 TEASPOON CHIPOTLE POWDER
1/2 FENNEL BULB, CUT INTO THIN SHAVINGS (FOR GARNISH)

DIRECTIONS

1. Blend all ingredients except the fennel shavings, until creamy (adding the water as needed and adjusting seasonings, especially the hot peppers, to taste).
2. Garnish with fennel and fresh ground pepper.

AVOCADO & CHIPOTLE BISQUE

Creamy avocados satiate hunger and satisfy the soul, and here they combine perfectly with cholesterol-reducing and metabolism-boosting spice. This soup makes for a beautiful and comforting presentation anytime.

INGREDIENTS

- **2** AVOCADOS, PITTED AND DICED (ROUGHLY 2 CUPS)
- **1** TABLESPOON OIL (HEMP, AVOCADO, OLIVE, FLAX)
- **1/4** CUP LIME JUICE
- **2** T WHITE MISO PASTE OR 1/2 TEASPOON COARSE SEA SALT
- **1 1/2** TEASPOONS FRESH ROSEMARY LEAVES OR 1/2 TEASPOON DRIED
- **1/2** TEASPOON CHIPOTLE POWDER
- **1** HANDFUL OF SPROUTS
- **1** HANDFUL OF SUNGOLDS (TOMATOES)

DIRECTIONS

1. Blend all together with 3 cups water (more or less depending on consistency), until smooth.
2. Divide into 4 servings.
3. Garnish each with some diced tomatoes, a sprig of rosemary, and sprouts.

SPICED PARSNIP SOUP

Parsnips are delicious and highly underrated. And they, like all root vegetables, ground and mineralize us.

INGREDIENTS

2 PARSNIPS, GRATED (IF ORGANIC, NO NEED TO PEEL)
2 TEASPOONS MACE
1/2 TEASPOON NUTMEG
1 TEASPOON CINNAMON
1 TABLESPOON LECITHIN
1 TEASPOON SEA SALT
2 TABLESPOONS RAW HONEY OR AGAVE (OR MAPLE SYRUP IS WONDERFUL IF YOU CAN GET IT LOCAL)
1 TABLESPOON LUCUMA
1 TABLESPOON MACA
2 TABLESPOONS COCONUT FLAKES, FINELY GROUND INTO A "FLOUR" IN A SPICE OR COFFEE GRINDER
PECANS (OPTIONAL)
DRIZZLE WITH MAPLE SYRUP FOR REAL TREAT AND SPRIGS OF FRESH ROSEMARY

DIRECTIONS

1. Grate the parsnips and put into a high speed blender or in a large bowl (if you're using a hand-held blender).
2. Grind the coconut flakes in a coffee or spice grinder and add to blender or bowl.
3. With 2 cups of water, begin blending the mixture, with all ingredients added until you have a delicious and creamy soup.
4. Ladle into individual bowls and serve with a drizzle of maple syrup and some chopped pecans if you want.

INGREDIENTS

4 RED PEPPERS, SEEDED AND CHOPPED
1 GARLIC CLOVE, PEELED AND MINCED
1 VIDALIA ONION, PEELED AND CHOPPED
1/4 CUP SUN-DRIED TOMATOES, SOAKED IN WATER UNTIL SOFT
1 TABLESPOON RAW HONEY OR AGAVE
1 TABLESPOON COLD-PRESSED OIL
1 CUP WATER
1/2 TEASPOON CHILI POWDER
1/2 TEASPOON OREGANO
1 TABLESPOON NUTRITIONAL YEAST
1 TABLESPOON MISO

DIRECTIONS

1. Puree until smooth.
2. Garnish with fresh black pepper & chili powder.

SOUTHERNBELLESIN LONDONSOUP

Does naming a soup after an indie rock song make it more fabulous? Maybe. But honestly, this soup needs no hype. Its delicious flavors are enough to make you rock out all on your own.

SPICY BLONDE

Rich and creamy, this soup only tastes sinfully rich. The spice adds just the right kick. The soup is equally apropos for being curled up at home or to serve at a dinner party.

INGREDIENTS

- **1/2** HEAD CAULIFLOWER, BROKEN INTO FLORETS ROUGHLY 1 INCH
- **1/4** CUP PINE NUTS (OPTIONAL)
- **2** CLOVES GARLIC, PEELED AND MINCED
- **2** TABLESPOONS RED WINE VINEGAR
- **1** SHALLOT, PEELED AND MINCED
- **1** ONION, PEELED AND CHOPPED
- **1** TEASPOON CHILI POWDER
- **1** TEASPOON CUMIN
- **1/2** TEASPOON CORIANDER SEEDS
- **1/4** TEASPOON TURMERIC
- **1** SMALL CUCUMBER, PEELED AND SEEDS DISCARDED, CHOPPED
- **2** TABLESPOONS COLD PRESSED OLIVE OIL (OR FLAX, AVOCADO, HEMP, ETC.)
- **1/2** CUP NUTRITIONAL YEAST
- SEA SALT AND PEPPER

DIRECTIONS

1. Blend all ingredients except cucumber in a high-speed blender (or in a large bowl with a hand-held blender) until smooth.
2. Garnish with diced cucumber and chili powder.

SMOKEY MUSHROOM MESQUITE SOUP

This really doesn't need much of an introduction. It's kinda delicious beyond words.

INGREDIENTS

2 CUPS MUSHROOMS (ANY VARIETY OR MIX OF DIFFERENT ONES YOU HAVE AVAILABLE), WITH 1/2 CUP RESERVED AND COARSELY CHOPPED
1/2 SWEET YELLOW ONION, LIKE VIDALIA, PEELED AND CHOPPED
1 HEAPING TABLESPOON MESQUITE
1 TABLESPOON BRAGG'S AMINO ACIDS OR NAMA SHOYU
1 TABLESPOON HEMP SEED BUTTER (OR ANY RAW NUT BUTTER)
1 CLOVE GARLIC, PEELED AND MINCED
1 TEASPOON APPLE CIDER VINEGAR
1 TEASPOON SEA SALT
1 TEASPOON PAPRIKA
A FEW SPRIGS OF FRESH ROSEMARY
2 CUPS WATER

DIRECTIONS

1. Blend all ingredients except the reserved 1/2 cup mushrooms which you can add to individual servings when the entire soup is blended and creamy.
2. In each bowl, sprinkle a few grains of coarse sea salt and fresh black pepper.

WINTERPEAR

Serve in martini glasses with thin slices of pears as garnish. Perfect for cold-weather festivities or dinner parties, using all of the amazing winter pear varieties.

INGREDIENTS

5 PEARS (WHATEVER VARIETY IS IN SEASON), CORED AND ROUGHLY CHOPPED (1 PEAR RESERVED AND CUT INTO THIN SLICES FOR THE GARNISH)
1/2 SWEET ONION (WALLA WALLA OR VIDALIA)
1 TABLESPOON RAW HONEY OR AGAVE
2 TEASPOONS GROUND CUMIN
2 CUPS WATER
1 TEASPOON SEA SALT
1 TEASPOON FRESH THYME OR 1/2 TEASPOON DRIED

DIRECTIONS

1. Blend until smooth.
2. Ladle into bowls and garnish with poppy seeds & a few thin pear slices.

NEW GARLIC SOUP

Whenever you're a bit under the weather or just want a simple (done in five minutes) and soothing broth, this soup is perfect. Simplicity is beauty.

INGREDIENTS

4 GREEN GARLIC BULBS (FRESH) OR YOU CAN USE 1 DRIED BULB, PEELED AND MINCED
2 CUPS WATER
1/2 CUP NUTRITIONAL YEAST
1 TABLESPOON MISO
  SEA SALT AND BLACK PEPPER TO TASTE
1 TEASPOON EACH: SAGE, THYME PARSLEY (FRESH OR DRIED)

DIRECTIONS

1. Blend until smooth.
2. Serve at room temperature, garnished with fresh parsley leaves.

INGREDIENTS

- **1** AVOCADO
- **2** CUPS WATER
- **1/2** ONION
- **2** LARGE TOMATOES, SEEDED AND CHOPPED
- **1** TABLESPOON SEA SALT
- **3/4** TEASPOON RED PEPPER POWDER
- **1/2** CLOVE MINCED GARLIC
- **1** TABLESPOON KELP POWDER
- **1** RED PEPPER
- **1** HANDFUL DULSE, SHREDDED (OR CUT WITH KITCHEN SHEARS)
- BLACK PEPPER TO TASTE
- **1** RED CHILI, SEEDED AND CHOPPED
- SCALLIONS TO GARNISH

DIRECTIONS

1. Blend together: avocado, water, onion, tomatoes, sea salt, red pepper powder, kelp powder and garlic.
2. Mix in with a spoon the dulse, chili and scallion pieces and fresh black pepper before serving in one large bowl that everyone can help themselves to or in small bowls.

CAJUN**CREOLE**

This rich, spicy soup will transport you right to 'Nawlins with each delicious sip!

BLOODY **MARY** SOUP

A soup that's reminiscent of your favorite cocktail? Yes, you heard that title right. This delicious soup has all of the traditional flavorings of a Bloody Mary, but without the energy-zapping alcohol! Enjoy.

FOR THE SOUP:

- 4 LARGE HEIRLOOM TOMATOES (PREFERABLY RED, BUT WITH HEIRLOOMS IT'S HARD TO RESIST THE BEAUTIFUL ODD COLORS, SO DON'T LIMIT YOURSELF. JUST SAVE A GREEN ONE FOR THE GARNISH), CHOPPED
- 1 HEAPING TABLESPOON HEMP SEED BUTTER
- 2 CUPS WATER
- 1 TABLESPOON SEA SALT
- 1 TEASPOON CELERY SALT
- 2 STALKS OF CELERY, ROUGHLY CHOPPED
- JUICE OF 1 FRESH LEMON
- 2 TEASPOONS CHILI POWDER (OR 1 SMALL RED CHILI, SEEDED AND CHOPPED), OR ADJUSTED TO YOUR PREFERRED LEVEL OF SPICE

FOR THE GARNISH:

- 1 STALK OF CELERY (LEAVES ATTACHED) FOR EACH SERVING
- 1/2 ONE RED ONION, MINCED
- 1 LARGE HEIRLOOM TOMATO (GREEN IF YOU CAN FIND THEM, AS THEY'RE THE PRETTIEST AND MOST STRIKING)
- 1 TABLESPOON GRATED LEMON ZEST
- 1 TABLESPOON FINELY CHOPPED FRESH GREEN CHILES, SEEDED (AGAIN, ADJUST TO YOUR PREFERRED LEVEL OF SPICE)

DIRECTIONS

1. Blend the soup ingredients until fairly smooth, it's okay if there are some celery chunks, adjusting the chili to your preference.
2. Pour into individual servings (either in larger bowls for

a main dish or in small shooters for an appetizer or elegant party).
3. Garnish each serving with a mix of the onion, green tomato, lemon zest and green chiles, with one leafy celery stalk to finish and a dash of fresh black pepper.

SHIITAKE **SWEET** AND **SOUR**

Earthy, succulent and the perfect combination of everyone's favorite flavors to dance in your mouth.

INGREDIENTS

- **2** HANDFULS SHIITAKE MUSHROOMS, 1/2 BLENDED AND 1/2 CHOPPED TO ADD AFTER
- **1** LARGE HANDFUL WOOD EAR MUSHROOMS (OR ANY COMBINATION OF WILD MUSHROOMS), 1/2 BLENDED AND 1/2 CHOPPED TO ADD AFTER
- **1** HEAPING TABLESPOON HEMP BUTTER
- **1** TEASPOON MISO PASTE
- **1** KNOB OF GINGER (ROUGHLY 1 INCH), PEELED AND MINCED OR SQUEEZED THROUGH A GARLIC PRESS
- **1** CLOVE GARLIC, PEELED AND MINCED
- **2** TABLESPOONS BRAGGS AMINO ACIDS
- **2** TABLESPOONS RAW HONEY OR AGAVE
- **2** TABLESPOONS NUTRITIONAL YEAST
- **1** TABLESPOON FRESH BASIL, MINCED
  SOME SHREDDED NAPA CABBAGE (OR ALREADY MADE SAUERKRAUT WITH NAPA)
- **3** STALKS OF GREEN ONIONS (SCALLIONS), MINCED
  A BUNCH OF FRESH CILANTRO LEAVES, MINCED
  A DRIZZLE OF CHILI OIL (OR POWDER) TO GARNISH
  ENOUGH WATER TO BLEND TO DESIRED CONSISTENCY
  BLACK PEPPER AND SEA SALT TO TASTE

DIRECTIONS

1. Blend 1/2 the mushrooms with the ginger juice (or minced pieces), garlic, bragg's, sweetener, nutritional yeast, and basil with enough water to make it the desired consistency.
2. Add the rest of the chopped mushrooms and sauerkraut or shredded cabbage.
3. Ladle into individual servings and garnish with scallions, cilantro, chopped nuts if you'd like, chili oil or powder, sea salt and pepper.
4. Savor the taste of the sweet forest.

PICADILLO SOUP

This is a cross between a salsa and a soup. Whatever it is, it's amazing beyond words!

INGREDIENTS

3 LARGE TOMATOES, ROUGHLY CHOPPED
1/2 RUTABAGA, SCRUBBED (OR PEELED) AND FINELY CHOPPED
2 CUPS SHIITAKE MUSHROOMS, COARSELY CHOPPED (WITH A FEW LEFT WHOLE TO ADD TO EACH SERVING)
1/2 YELLOW SWEET ONION, PEELED AND CHOPPED (SOME FINELY AND SOME MORE COARSELY)
1 RED BELL PEPPER, COARSELY CHOPPED WITH SEEDS REMOVED
1/4 CUP OLIVES (ANY KIND, GREEN/BLACK/KALAMATA, AND IF YOU'RE NOT USING CAPERS USE 1/2- 1 WHOLE CUP), PITTED AND CHOPPED
1/2 CUP RAISINS (ANY VARIETY: FLAME, THOMPSON, GOLDEN, OR A MIX OF ALL 3)
2 TABLESPOONS CAPERS

1 CLOVE GARLIC, PEELED AND MINCED (IN GARLIC PRESS IF POSSIBLE)
1 HEAPING TABLESPOON NUTRITIONAL YEAST
1 TABLESPOON FRESH OREGANO OR 1 TEASPOON DRIED
2 TEASPOONS PAPRIKA
2 TEASPOON CHIPOTLE POWDER
1 TABLESPOON BRAGGS AMINO ACIDS OR NAMA SHOYU
1 TABLESPOON APPLE CIDER OR UMEBOSHI PLUM VINEGAR
1 TEASPOON CUMIN
1/2 TEASPOON MESQUITE POWDER (IF YOU HAVE IT, IT'S OKAY TO LEAVE IT OUT)
2 CUPS WATER (OR ENOUGH TO CREATE A SOUPY CONSISTENCY)
SALT AND PEPPER TO TASTE

DIRECTIONS

1. Mash all ingredients around for a few squeezes with your hands until it's more liquid than a salsa, but still pretty chunky.
2. Let sit for as long as possible for the flavors to marinate deliciously, but it can also be eaten right away; it's so appealing and fresh that it might be hard to wait!

JAMAICAN STEW

A mashed up flavor cacophony: sweet, salty, tangy and creamy. Start a dance party in your mouth!

INGREDIENTS

- **1/2** WHOLE PINEAPPLE, PEELED AND CHOPPED
- **2** AVOCADOS, PITTED AND CHOPPED
- **1** TABLESPOON CURRY POWDER
- **1** TEASPOON THYME
- **1** LARGE GARLIC CLOVE, PEELED AND MINCED
- **1** LARGE ONION, PEELED AND DICED
- **1** TABLESPOON CRUSHED RED PEPPER
- **1** TEASPOON ALLSPICE
- **2** TABLESPOONS APPLE CIDER VINEGAR
- **1/4** CUP CAPERS
  - TOMATOES
  - CILANTRO TO GARNISH
  - CORN AND PEAS (LEFT WHOLE)
- **1** TEASPOON SEA SALT
  - BLACK PEPPER TO GARNISH
- **1-2** CUPS WATER, TO CREATE THE SOUP CONSISTENCY YOU WANT

DIRECTIONS

1. In a large bowl or high speed blender pulse briefly: pineapple, avocado, curry powder, thyme, garlic, onion, red pepper, allspice, apple cider vinegar, tomatoes and sea salt with the water (adding slowly until it's the desired consistency).
2. Add the capers, corn and peas to the coarse and chunky mixture.
3. Season with black pepper and cilantro leaves.

WINTER**WARMING**CHILI

Using the meatballs from Raw Food, Fast Food, this chili is incredible and satisfying—perfect for all those "meat lovers" out there who feel like vegan and especially raw meals won't satiate them. Oh how happy they'll be to be proven wrong!

FOR THE MEATBALLS:

4 TABLESPOONS NUTRITIONAL YEAST
2 TABLESPOON MESQUITE
1 TABLESPOON MAPLE SYRUP
1 TABLESPOON MACA
1 TABLESPOON HEMP SEED BUTTER
1/2 ONION, PEELED AND FINELY DICED
1/2 TEASPOON EACH: CUMIN, MARJORAM, PEPPER, NUTMEG, OREGANO, ALLSPICE, CAYENNE PEPPER, CHIPOTLE, GINGER (FRESH MINCED OR GROUND POWDER), PAPRIKA
1 TABLESPOON EACH: DRIED BASIL, THYME, SAGE

DIRECTIONS

1. Mix all ingredients together in a bowl with a spoon or your fingers.
2. When it's all combined and sticky, break off tablespoon size pieces and instead of packing firmly, just gently and quickly mash into meatballs, leaving them looking rough for a "meaty" texture.

FOR THE CHILI:

1 RED ONION, PEELED AND CHOPPED
1 GREEN PEPPER, SEEDED AND CHOPPED
2 GARLIC CLOVES, PEELED AND MINCED
1 SMALL JALAPENO PEPPER, SEEDED AND CHOPPED
4 LARGE HEIRLOOM TOMATOES, SEEDED AND COARSELY CHOPPED
4 SOFT DATES, PITTED AND CHOPPED FINELY (FOR EASY BLENDING)

1 TABLESPOON APPLE CIDER VINEGAR
1 TABLESPOON RAW HONEY OR AGAVE
1 TABLESPOON CHILI POWDER
1 TEASPOON CUMIN POWDER
1 TEASPOON OREGANO
FRESHLY GROUND PEPPER
COARSE SEA SALT

DIRECTIONS

1. Mix all ingredients together roughly so it's a chunky and ever so slightly soupy mess.
2. Add the "meatballs" and plunk down on the table for everyone to dig into!

AVOCADO SOUP

Creamy and ready in minutes. It's hard to go wrong with this one, and the variations are endless, as it's essentially the base for most other creamy raw soups!

INGREDIENTS
1 AVOCADO, PITTED AND PEELED
1 CUCUMBER, SEEDED AND PEELED
1/2 CUP WATER (OR ENOUGH TO BLEND)
JUICE OF 1 LEMON
1 TEASPOON (OR MORE TO TASTE) SEA SALT
FRESHLY GROUND BLACK PEPPER
1/2 GARLIC CLOVE, PEELED AND MINCED

DIRECTIONS

1. Blend until smooth and creamy, serve immediately or keep in fridge until ready to eat.

SUMMER COOLER SOUPS

GAZPACHO **WITH** CUMIN **AND** AVOCADO

A summertime classic. Raw foodists and non-raw foodists alike are accustomed to making this soup all the time!

INGREDIENTS

- **2** AVOCADOS, PITTED AND CHOPPED
- **2** LARGE HEIRLOOM TOMATOES, SEEDED AND DICED
- **1** MEDIUM CUCUMBER, DICED
- **1** RED ONION, PEELED AND FINELY DICED
- **1** CUP FRESH CORN
- **3** GREEN ONIONS, FINELY DICED
- JUICE OF 1 LIME
- **2** TABLESPOONS RED WINE OR APPLE CIDER VINEGAR
- **1** TEASPOON MESQUITE POWDER
- **2** TEASPOONS RAW HONEY OR AGAVE
- **1** TABLESPOON BRAGG'S AMINO ACIDS OR NAMA SHOYU
- **1** TEASPOON SEA (OR HIMALAYAN) SALT
- **1/2** TEASPOON GROUND GINGER
- JUICE AND CHOPPED UP PULP OF 1 ORANGE
- **1/4** TEASPOON GROUND CLOVES
- **1** TEASPOON GROUND CUMIN
- **1** GARLIC CLOVE, PEELED AND MINCED (IN A GARLIC PRESS IF POSSIBLE)
- BLACK PEPPER TO TASTE

DIRECTIONS

1. Blend the avocado, tomatoes, cucumber, onion, lime and orange juice, cloves, cumin, garlic, salt, braggs, honey, mesquite, and vinegar together until creamy, adding some water if necessary.
2. Add the corn, green onions and black pepper and serve.

SUMMER**MINESTRONE**

A classic soup to use up the garden's bounty. Mmmm.

INGREDIENTS

1 TEASPOON OIL
1 YELLOW ONION, PEELED AND CHOPPED
1/2 BUNCH FRESH OREGANO OR 2 TEASPOONS DRIED
2 CLOVES GARLIC, PEELED AND MINCED
4 YELLOW SQUASH, CHOPPED
2 ZUCCHINI, CHOPPED
2 CARROTS, CHOPPED
2 EARS OF FRESH CORN OR 1/2 PACKAGE FROZEN ORGANIC CORN
4 LARGE TOMATOES, SEEDED AND CHOPPED
4 CUPS WATER
2 TABLESPOONS NUTRITIONAL YEAST
1 TABLESPOON BRAGGS OR NAMA SHOYU
1 BUNCH SPINACH OR 4 CUPS LOOSE LEAVES
1 HEAPING TEASPOON SEA SALT
FRESHLY GROUND PEPPER

DIRECTIONS

1. Pulse half of all vegetables with the rest of the ingredients in the blender (or with a hand-held in a large bowl) until coarsely pureed, leaving some chunks.
2. Pour into bowls.
3. Ladle the rest of the chopped vegetables into each serving and garnish with black pepper and any fresh herbs you like.

CHILLED ZUCCHINI SOUP

Absolutely beautiful and so easy.

INGREDIENTS

2 TABLESPOONS COLD PRESSED OLIVE OIL (OR YOUR CHOICE)
1 YELLOW ONION, PEELED AND CHOPPED
1 LARGE GARLIC CLOVE, PEELED AND CHOPPED
1/2 TEASPOON DRIED THYME LEAVES OR 1 TEASPOON FRESH
6 ZUCCHINI, ROUGHLY PEELED. LEAVE A FEW LONG SLICES (WITH THE PEEL INTACT) FOR GARNISH
  SEA SALT
3 CUPS WATER
1 HEAPING TABLESPOON FRESH BASIL LEAVES
  FRESH GROUND PEPPER
2 GIANT HANDFULS ARUGULA OR PURSLANE, RESERVED FOR INDIVIDUAL SERVINGS

DIRECTIONS

1. Puree all ingredients except the greens and zucchini garnish.
2. Garnish individual servings with the arugula (or purslane) and slices of zucchini.

CORN, AVOCADO AND BASIL CHOWDER

Creamy and comforting, but light enough to be absolutely perfect for a hot summer day.

INGREDIENTS

- **1** YELLOW ONION, PEELED AND DICED
- **1** CLOVE GARLIC, PEELED AND MINCED
- **2** CUPS CORN
- **1/4** CUP NUTRITIONAL YEAST
- **1** TABLESPOON SEA SALT
- **1** RED PEPPER, SEEDED AND DICED (1/2 FOR BLENDING AND 1/2 FOR MIXING IN AFTER)
  MEAT AND WATER FROM 1 YOUNG THAI COCONUT OR 2 TABLESPOONS HEMP BUTTER AND 1 CUP WATER
- **2** TEASPOONS KELP POWDER FOR THE OCEAN FLAVOR
- **1** AVOCADO, PITTED
  A FEW SPRIGS OF FRESH BASIL

DIRECTIONS

1. Blend onion, garlic, corn, nutritional yeast, salt, 1/2 of the red pepper, coconut meat and water (or hemp and water) and kelp powder until creamy.
2. Garnish with avocado slices, the other 1/2 of red pepper, and shredded basil leaves.

FRESH**BERRY**SOUP

Bright, colorful, rich and dessert-like. Looks beautiful in any bowl or glass.

INGREDIENTS

- **3** PLUMS, PITTED AND CHOPPED
- **2** PEACHES, PITTED AND CHOPPED
- **1** CUP RASPBERRIES
- **1** CUP HALVED STRAWBERRIES
- **1** YOUNG THAI COCONUT, MEAT AND WATER
- JUICE OF 1 ORANGE
- **1** TABLESPOON RAW HONEY OR AGAVE
- JUICE OF 1 LEMON
- **1** TEASPOON VANILLA EXTRACT
- **1** TEASPOON GROUND CINNAMON
- **1** PINCH GROUND CLOVES

DIRECTIONS

1. Blend all ingredients, saving a small handful of the chopped pieces of each of the fruits, adding to the soup at the end for delicious chunkiness.

TOMATO BASIL SOUP

If you can't get fresh heirloom tomatoes from a garden or farmer's market, it's best to wait to make this recipe until you can. Mealy, store-bought tomatoes that have been shipped from California just won't cut it.

INGREDIENTS
4 CUPS CHOPPED TOMATOES (ANY VARIETY)
1/4 CUP COLD PRESSED OIL (FLAX, OLIVE, AVOCADO, HEMP)
1 TABLESPOON RAW HONEY OR AGAVE
1/2 CUP BASIL LEAVES, CHOPPED

DIRECTIONS
1. Blend 3/4 of the tomatoes with the oil, sweetener and 2 cups of water until smooth.
2. Pour into 4 bowls.
3. Add 1/4 cup of remaining chopped tomatoes with the strips of basil (divided between the servings) and serve.

INGREDIENTS

- 1 MEDIUM CUCUMBER, PEELED IF NON-ORGANIC, OTHERWISE JUST CHOPPED
- 1 AVOCADO, PITTED
- A HANDFUL OF FRESH PARSLEY
- 2 TEASPOONS PAPRIKA
- 2 CUPS WATER
- 1 CLOVE GARLIC, PEELED AND MINCED
- 2 TEASPOONS RAW HONEY OR AGAVE

DIRECTIONS

1. Blend until smooth and creamy.
2. Garnish with some thin slices of cucumbers.

SWEET **CHILLED** AVOCADO **CUCUMBER** AND **PAPRIKA** SOUP

An absolutely delicious and creamy blend with a hint of summery spice. This whips up in a flash, yet works perfectly for company as well.

AUGUST SUNSET

Eating this soup is like eating the sunshine as it sets glorious. It's a perfect end to a summer evening or even when the days begin to cool a bit.

INGREDIENTS

2 GARLIC CLOVES, PEELED AND MINCED
1 TABLESPOON MISO
4 LARGE YELLOW HEIRLOOM TOMATOES
2 HANDFULS SUNGOLDS (OR ANY SMALL CHERRY TOMATO), HALVED
1 YELLOW PEPPER, SEEDED AND CHOPPED
1 VIDALIA (OR ANY SWEET YELLOW ONION) PEELED AND CHOPPED
1 CUP FRESH OR FROZEN CORN
1/2 BUNCH YELLOW BASIL LEAVES
   SEA SALT
1 LEMON, ZEST AND JUICE
2 TEASPOONS CHILI PEPPER

DIRECTIONS

1. Blend all ingredients except the chervil, tarragon, basil and a handful of reserved sungolds (halved).
2. Garnish the individual servings with the above and savor.

INGREDIENTS:

Fruits and Vegetables

Here are some simple tips to help you select and work with produce:

- Buy **ORGANIC** and local/seasonal whenever you can.

- If you can't find organic produce, make sure you're **WASHING** well and/or **PEELING** them.

- Eat lots of **GREEN LEAFY VEGETABLES** in any way you can: in green smoothies, juices, salads, or just munching on them as snacks. Kale chips, for example, are a terrific way of getting greens in as a simple and portable snack. There are some really delicious dehydrated kale chips on the market, particularly from www.BestRawFoodStore.com, so if you don't have access to your own dehydrator, check them out. Green vegetables in any form are better than none at all, and many of the healthy elements, such as chlorophyll, minerals, potassium, etc., are heat sensitive and are destroyed (along with the enzymes) by cooking.

- Don't forget about the **WILD GREENS** either! Often found right in your backyard or in neighborhood alleyways and roadsides (before you forage, find out about spraying patterns in the area). Dandelion greens are a great example. Appearing in the spring, they are a vibrant and potent wild food with a hearty life force that builds healthy blood and detoxifies the body—and yet most people view them as a pesky weed to be gotten rid of! You'll be doing everyone, most of all yourself, a favor by picking and eating them!

- All fruits and vegetables are incredibly **HYDRATING**. As you enter this lifestyle, this will cut down on your need to be constantly guzzling water. **CUCUMBERS** and **CELERY** are especially hydrating: they also replace natural salt reserve, help to grow strong hair and nails, and contain natural cooling properties in summer months.

- **JICAMA** is used in several of the recipes here. If you're not familiar with it, it's a root vegetable from Mexico that's low in calories, high in water content, and high in vitamin C. Supermarkets carry it year round, so it's possible to enjoy its versatility in every season.

- You'll notice that **LEMONS** are used in almost all of the recipes here. They're also a main component of the healthiest morning ritual: drink a glass of room temperature filtered or spring water with freshly squeezed lemon juice. This will improve lymph and circulation, rejuvenate the liver, and provide your body with necessary calcium. If you use a lovely organic, sun-ripened lemon, it will provide your body with over 200 enzymes, which is a fabulous way to start your day!

- There's some debate about **ONIONS, GARLIC, LEEKS** and **CHIVES**, but in my opinion, they grow on this earth for a purpose and have very powerful medicinal value, even and maybe especially when consumed raw. They all contain enzymes that enhance carcinogenic excretion, which helps protect against cancer. (1) In our world today, we can definitely use all the cancer fighting properties we can get our hands on! In addition, they add delicious flavor and quick crunch to many savory recipes without fat or calories. I personally can't get enough of garlic, and I usually eat a few cloves a day!

- Also, it seems that onions are also rich in **HISTADINE**, an important element in attaining orgasms. (2) Enough said.

- Another note regarding **ONIONS** and **GARLIC**: Consuming them along with raw apple cider vinegar activates their allicin content. **ALLICIN** is an oil that clear the blood and "boosts enzymatic activity, moving sluggish fecal matter from the colon, and dislodging accumulated waste in the digestive tract." (3)

Seaweeds

In this book, I use the following varieties of sea vegetables (although there are definitely many more): nori, dulse and kelp (in powder, flake and noodle form).

These seaweeds and sea vegetables contain all necessary trace minerals and nutrients that our bodies need for optimal functioning. Sea vegetables are actually around twelve times more nutritious than the average vegetable, with high amounts of iodine (to regulate metabolism and thyroid functioning), B6, B12, and magnesium. Brown seaweeds in particular contain fucoxanthin, which is thought to promote weight loss by stimulating a protein that burns "the visceral fat that surrounds internal organs in the abdomen- the type of fat linked to heart disease, diabetes and metabolic syndrome."(4) This is definitely a good thing. Seaweeds also stimulate the liver to produce essential fatty acids that keep our brains functioning at optimal levels—also a good thing!

Today, as the earth's topsoil becomes a highly endangered commodity, it's more important than ever to use the abundant vegetables of our nutrient rich oceans, not just for our health, but for our precious home planet. (5)

IRISH MOSS Used as a thickening agent after rinsing and soaking, this sea vegetable is highly mineralized and aids in soothing the entire digestive tract.

SPIRULINA One of the highest plant-based sources of protein, this blue green algae boasts lots of amino acids that break down for maximum assimilation. Slightly sweet and easily blended into any recipe or sprinkled on salads, it is 60% protein (as compared to animal flesh, which is only about 27%). (6) It's also the highest source of vitamin B 12, as well as A, B1, B2, D, E and K, with chlorophyll and vital trace minerals, elements, cell salts and enzymes. (7)

For those who are looking to lose weight, spirulina helps curb the appetite while giving our bodies the complete nutrition we need to be vibrantly energetic.

Superfoods

MACA is an earthy, sweet, mildly spicy addition to many recipes. It's derived from Tuberose root (related to the radish) from South America. It contains "four alkaloids that have been proven to nourish the body's endocrine's glands and the glandular functions, promoting hormonal balance and aiding the reproductive system in both women and men. It's rich in calcium, magnesium, and iron and contains trace minerals such as zinc, iodine, selenium, copper and manganese as well as B vitamins." (8)

Maca has been used in traditional South American diets to support brain function and the endocrine system, to increase energy, endurance, stamina, work as a libido enhancer and natural aphrodisiac, and to regulate menstrual cycles. It is an overall adaptogen, which means that it works on whatever the body needs fixed!

MESQUITE comes from an Argentinean tree, and its meal comes from the ground pods. This superfood has a delicious smoky and slightly sweet flavor that proves distinct and versatile in both sweet and savory recipes. It's a powerful staple in traditional Native American diets, especially in desert areas. It contains incredibly high amounts of protein, calcium, and many other minerals like magnesium, iron, potassium and zinc. It also contains lots of fiber and is low in natural sugars.

HEMP SEEDS (We mainly use it in the form of seed-butter in this book). An important staple in the lives of our ancestors, hemp has been called—not without justification—the "elixir of immortality." It's used in many cultures as a perfect source of food, fuel and textile fiber.

In case you're wondering (and I know you are) hemp is a cousin to marijuana, but not the same plant, as is commonly assumed. Hemp seeds do not contain THC! They are, though, incredibly nutritious and powerful. Hemp is a complete protein, closely resembling human blood plasma, so it can be absorbed and utilized by the body easily. It's full of antioxidants, contains a complete balance of essential fatty acids, and many inflammation fighting properties.

Make sure the hemp seeds you're getting are raw and shelled; hemp seeds in the shell are usually heat-treated to stop the germination process, and all healing properties are destroyed.

We use hemp butter in many of these recipes because of its health benefits, but also to support the growth and cultivation of such a wonderfully beneficial and eco-friendly crop. Using hemp, rather than nuts, is also a simple and delicious way to make as many recipes nut-free as possible.

There are lots of brands out there; just be sure to look for raw and unheated (available in most health food stores and all the raw online sources at the back of the book).

NB: Hemp butter tends to have an earthy, substantial taste, so I sometimes mix a bit of honey or agave and some sea salt into the jar, or just adjust the recipes to accommodate tastes.

SESAME SEEDS When you consume sesame seeds raw and un-hulled, you get much more of their calcium and nutrients, along with their beneficial properties for liver function and blood sugar balance.(9)

Sesame seeds can also be made more digestible by blending into a paste or "butter" like tahini (savory) or adding some stevia, honey or agave for a sweeter "nut butter" replacement.

A note about all the nut butters taking the place of peanuts and peanut butter: peanut butter is ubiquitous in our culture, but peanuts are actually a highly toxic legume, full of mold/fungus, and in the heating process their oils are turned into dangerous free radicals and are known to cause many health problems (least of which is the fact that peanuts turn into immoveable sludge in our intestines). It's best to only consume the wild jungle/organic peanuts. (See Sources for more information, as www.BestRawFoodStore.com and Sunfood Nutrition both carry the real wild peanuts).

SEA SALT AND HIMALAYAN SALT The salt seen commonly on our tables is a less than optimal choice for many reasons. The first is that our bodies are forced to use a huge amount of water just to neutralize the salt's toxins and dehydrating properties. This causes excess and unhealthy fluid to be produced in the body tissue and leads directly to an abundance of cellulite, arthritis issues, and kidney and gall stones, just to name a few. Commercially produced salt also wreaks havoc on the environment, and toxic chemicals are used in its production (and subsequently in the product that ends up on people's dining tables).

Real sea salt or Himalayan salt enhances flavor, aids digestion, flushes toxins, and provides essential minerals in our bodies, so it's important to keep these two kinds of salt in our diets. In general, look for slightly moist, grayish color and a coarsely ground texture. Sea salt is available at all health food stores and most supermarkets nowadays; Himalayan salt can also be found in health food stores or online. Most of the companies listed in the sources section carry both varieties.

These amazingly potent salts contain all eighty-four of the trace elements that are found in our bodies. They regulate our natural water balance and pH balance in our cells, healthy blood sugar, energy levels, food absorption, respiratory and intestinal health, bone strength, properly functioning libido, heart support and blood pressure regulation. They can aid in reducing muscle cramps and curing insomnia.

Celtic, or Atlantic Sea Salt, is damp and a dirty, grayish color. Himalayan salt is either a gorgeous pink crystal-looking color or rich, black and earthy, with a strong sulfur smell (also very healthy for our bodies). Make sure you're finding traditional and slowly sun-dried salt, which preserves the vital enzymes, minerals and trace elements. We want to make sure nothing is lost in the heating process, such as magnesium, a huge detoxifier that's never present in regular table salt. Magnesium is also necessary in the salt we're getting because it has the added benefit of helping to digest simple sugars, so if you are ever consuming refined carbs, fats, starches and proteins, real sun-dried salt will allow the body to process them with ease. (10)

While you can definitely use the extract, make sure it's organic (commercial brands put corn syrup and other fillers into their extracts), and/or maybe even make your own liquid extract from soaking the whole beans in a tiny amount of alcohol. If you can buy the beans whole and scrape the seeds out to use in recipes, do, as the flavor is unmatched. Powders are also available and are useful for dissolving in liquids or adding to cake or cookie type recipes. Again, make sure you're using organic if possible. When buying vanilla beans, hold them to the light and look for sparkling crystals on the beans, as it means they're very high quality and have lots of sexy vanilla flavor.

Herbs and Spices

TURMERIC Antioxidant, used especially when around low frequency electromagnetic waves (in cities especially)

CINNAMON The bark of this aromatic plant is one of the oldest spices known, slightly sweet, high in antioxidants, antimicrobial, normalizes blood sugar levels, contains iron, calcium, manganese, treats diarrhea and digestive problems. (13)

GINGER Increases blood flow, keeps extremities warm, keeps body warm in cold weather, soothing to digestion and stomach (14)

PARSLEY Chromium to help cope with sugars, manage weight, maximize muscle and fitness potential, important for cardiovascular and cholesterol health (15)

BASIL Anti- bacterial properties, providing hygiene to the body, clears parasites, and sedates muscles. Cleanses kidneys and liver, contains chlorophyll, vitamin A and C. (16)

BURDOCK ROOT Wild food with great tonifying, strengthening, detoxifying energy and properties, maintains hair color and healthy skin, blood cell formations, metabolism of proteins and fats, produces folic acid, rich in hormones and minerals (17)

Sweeteners

STEVIA Very, very sweet (300x stronger than regular sugar), highly concentrated, stevia is derived from a South American herb. It has no glycemic index, so it's safe for children and diabetics. Available as the whole leaf, powder, liquid and now even tablet form.

MAPLE SYRUP Not a raw sweetener but it's a beautifully traditional process, where sap is gathered from maple trees and boiled down to a thick liquid. Use sparingly, as it holds a strong and sweet flavor.

HONEY Full of enzymes, adds to our enzyme reserves, which very few other foods do, also sucrose, a beneficial sugar. It's best derived from wildflower or fruit sources, rather than grain. Make sure it's semi solid so you know it hasn't been heated. In my opinion it's one of the best foods on the planet.

AGAVE From the plant that blue agave tequila comes from, long used for food, drink and fiber, 90% fructose, 10% glucose. Natural fructose has a very low glycemic value, so it's safe for diabetics and children or anyone with sensitivity to sugar. . . Processed naturally so it's safer than any chemical fructose, and is easily used in liquids or recipes.

BRAGG'S AMINO ACIDS OR NAMA SHOYU This fermented soy product (the only type of soy I recommend) contains lots of essential and beneficial amino acids made from cultured soybeans and aged, sometimes for years. It's full of beneficial enzymes.

DRIED FRUITS Drying (dehydrating) fruit takes the water out and concentrates the food, giving it more substance, energy, sweetness and flavor, and making it perfect for snacking or traveling. Just be careful not to overdo it with dried fruits, as they are really concentrated in (natural) sugars, and buy organic, unsulphured, unsweetened fruits. They keep best in the fridge, and can also be soaked for easier blending and digestibility.

The dried fruits used most frequently here (and in many raw foodist's menu plans) are dates; an ancient and cultivated since the beginning of civilization food staple. Dates are full of natural sugars and energy; very, very sweet, high in fiber, carbohydrates and more potassium than bananas, B vitamins, magnesium, iron (for feeding the cells in our body). (18)

NUTRITIONAL YEAST Used as a replacement for parmesan cheese in a lot of my recipes, nutritional yeast is high in B-complex vitamins, among many others, and is available (usually in bulk) at any health food store and often larger supermarkets. It has a savory, cheese-like flavor, and a consistency (when added to liquids) that's delicious.

COCONUT BUTTER Full of weight-loss and energy boosting properties, pure and extra virgin coconut oil is a firm "butter" when at room temperature, but turns into liquid oil at the melting point of 70 degrees F. It helps with metabolism and thyroid function, contains medium-chain fatty acids to aid in weight loss and the metabolism of fats, has antibacterial and anti-fungal properties, balances cholesterol, and is used to add creaminess and nutrition to recipes. It's also the most amazing skin moisturizer available, with an incredibly edible and exotic aroma. I use it daily.

YOUNG THAI COCONUTS Your best bet for finding a Young Thai Coconut will be Whole Foods or a local Asian market. But more and more health food stores and supermarkets are now carrying them. They are different than the mature brown round coconuts: they are white (after the green husk has been taken off), and while cracking them open can be an involved process, with just a few practice rounds (and a large, blunt knife), you'll be breaking into them like a pro in no time and harvesting the incredible and delicious young coconut meat and delicious water within.

The water is very similar to human blood plasma and was used in the South Pacific during the WW's in blood transfusions. It's low in calories and basically fat-free—nature's own perfect source of electrolytes—making it the perfect recovery liquid for athletes or anyone in a really hot climate. It helps the gall bladder, liver, kidney and thyroid functions (19).

Fermented Foods

Fermented foods are important for many reasons, mainly because of the way they heal our digestive tracts. They are twice as easily digested as other foods, due to their production and live active cultures. There are three fermented foods that I use frequently in this book, but I've listed others as well and highly recommend getting as many fermented products into your daily diet as possible for optimal health.

MISO is fermented soybeans, rice spores (koji), and/or chickpeas. Miso is a living food, full of enzymes and comparable only to bee pollen for its easily assimilated protein content. It's perfect for healing diets, a wonderful digestive and appetite stimulant, and heals the digestive tract.

APPLE CIDER VINEGAR This raw vinegar still contains the "mother" of live active cultures. It stands apart from all other vinegars because, unlike the pasteurized and de-natured ones that are toxic and mineral-depleted, raw apple cider vinegar actually promotes vibrant health and proper pH balance in the body. Made by crushing organic (and unheated) apples in wooden barrels, and then leaving it to mature and ferment, you can tell that apple cider vinegar is alive and whole if it has the cloudy reddish brown substance called the "mother" floating in the bottle. Raw apple cider vinegar contains potassium, calcium, magnesium, phosphorous, chlorine, sodium, sulfur, copper, iron, silicon and fluorine that are essential for vibrant health. Look for brands like Spectrum, Eden, Westbrae Naturals and Bragg's, to help fight bacteria, reduce sinus infections, soothe sore throats, allergies and muscle fatigue, as well as improve digestion, constipation and even food poisoning. Apple cider vinegar also balances cholesterol levels, strengthens immunity and stamina, increases metabolism and is therefore perfect as we age and our systems need extra support. To wit, it also helps with degenerative problems such as arthritis and gout, bladder stones, and UTI's.

SAUERKRAUT Basically shredded vegetables (usually cabbage with a mix of beets, carrots, radishes, etc.), sauerkraut is full of predigested proteins and sugars, loaded with enzymes, and an overall perfect food for digestion. Cabbage contains vitamin U, which heals the digestive tract, restores pH levels, and keeps vital and healthy intestinal bacteria flourishing. Sauerkraut has been used all over the world through the ages, and is considered by all cultures (no pun intended) to be one of the most important foods we consume. Every culture and traditional medicinal system basically believes that an absence of good intestinal bacteria (flora) is at the root of all disease.

The great thing about sauerkraut is that it's exceptionally cheap and really easy to make, especially when compared to store-bought acidophilus products, whose actual benefit is questionable due to processing, packaging and shelf-life.

Some other fermented products that I didn't include in these recipes, but highly recommend that you seek out and use in your daily diet, are: **KOMBUCHA, KEFIR, RAW SEED YOGURTS** and **CHEESE**. All of these help keep the colon slightly acidic which is key to vibrant health and a strong immune system, preventing and even healing many diseases.

"When you consume fermented foods, you will have the most amazing unblemished skin, a vital immune system, a healthy colon, a good disposition, good digestive health, endurance, environmental tolerance, a thin waist, excellent healthy stools, ease during the ovulation cycle and healthy joints." (20)

REFERENCES:

1. **ANNIE PADDEN JUBB AND DAVID JUBB**, Life Force Nutrition
   (North Atlantic Books, 2003)

2, 3, 5, 6, 7, 9, 10, 14, 15, 16, 20 **JUBB AND JUBB**, Life Force Nutrition

4. **DR. ANDREW WEIL** (www.drweil.com)

8. **MATTHEW ROGERS AND TIZIANA ALIPO TAMBORRA**, Sweet Gratitude: A New World of Raw Desserts (North Atlantic Publishing, 2008)

13, 17, 18, **ROGERS AND TAMBORRA**, A New World

19. **SARMA MELNGAILIS AND MATTHEW KENNEY**, Raw Food Real World
    (Harper Collins, 2005)

YOUR NOTES:

SOURCES:

Your best source for most ingredients used in this book are your local farmer's market, health food store, (even larger grocery chains carry lots of organic staples, if that's your primary shopping option), and yours (or your friends') gardens.

Since most recipes are focused on fruits and vegetables, spices, herbs and bulk items, I think it's really important to support your small local businesses, farms and/or to grow your own food as much as possible.

However, I also am a fan of superfoods and a few harder-to-find items that you can buy from the online sources below. They will last a really long time, getting you through all of these recipes and beyond!

Here are some of my favorite online stores with raw, organic and the highest quality products:

Best Raw Food Store (www.bestrawfoodstore.com) For an enormous selection of raw food staples, including all the superfoods such as maca, mesquite, lucuma, hemp butter (and the highest quality raw nut butters), Himalayan and sea salt, as well as a great selection of books, lifestyle and supplemental products, and even packaged raw goodies to try!

Maine Sea Coast Vegetables (http://www.seaveg.com), for all sea vegetables harvested sustainably off the coast of Maine.

Mountain Rose Herbs (http://www.mountainroseherbs.com) The highest quality spices and herbs, even bulk teas and oils, if you can't find them locally or homegrown.

One Lucky Duck (http://www.oneluckyduck.com) For superfoods, some sea vegetable, raw honey, salt and other miscellaneous ingredients, as well as an incredible selection of simply decadent/vegan beauty products for everyone who wants to glow!

Sunfood Nutrition (http://www.sunfood.com) Superfoods, raw ingredient staples, high quality sun dried olives, fruits and truly raw nuts, etc.

SweetLeaf Stevia (http://www.sweetleaf.com/) for stevia products, especially the flavored liquid drops.

Since the only piece of equipment you need for these recipes is a blender, and most everyone has one already, there's really no need to source any pieces of equipment, but if you're looking for a really do-all sort of blender, you might want to consider a Vita-Mix (www.vitamix.com) or check out Craigslist, Amazon, or any online kitchen supply company for something to mix all your wonderful creations up in.

BOOK RECOMMENDATIONS:

RAW FOOD, FAST FOOD by Philip McCluskey

RAW FOOD JUICE BAR by Philip McCluskey

DETOX YOUR WORLD by Shazzie

THE SUNFOOD DIET SUCCESS SYSTEM by David Wolfe

EVIE'S KITCHEN by Shazzie

GREEN FOR LIFE by Victoria Boutenko

WWW.LOVINGRAW.COM

RECIPE BOOKS

Check out my latest recipes books now available online:
www.lovingraw.com

RAW FOOD, FAST FOOD
&
RAW FOOD SALAD BAR

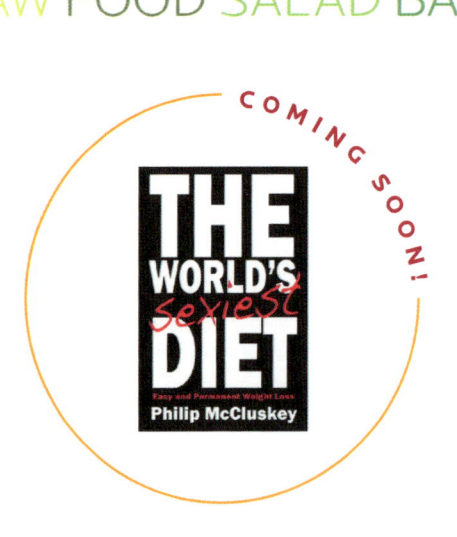

COMING SOON!

THE WORLD'S sexiest DIET
Easy and Permanent Weight Loss
Philip McCluskey

Made in the USA
Charleston, SC
08 June 2012